Coaching Youth Soccer

Third Edition

American Sport Education Program

Human Kinetics

Library of Congress Cataloging-in-Publication Data

Coaching youth soccer / American Sport Education Program.--3rd ed.
p. cm.
ISBN 0-7360-3718-7
1. Soccer for children--Coaching. 2. Soccer--Coaching. I. American Sport Education Program.
GV943.8.C63 2001
796.334'07'7--dc21 00-050032

ISBN: 0-7360-3718-7

Acquisitions Editor: Thomas Hanlon; **Games Consultant**: John Croumbe-Liley; **Developmental Editor**: Leigh LaHood; **Copyeditor**: Bonnie Pettifor; **Proofreader**: Myla Smith; **Graphic Designer**: Fred Starbird; **Graphic Artist**: Sandra Meier; **Cover Designer**: Jack W. Davis; **Photographer (cover and interior)**: Tom Roberts; **Illustrators**: Sharon Smith and Tom Roberts (Mac art); Roberto Sabas (line drawings); **Printer**: United Graphics

Copies of this book are available at special discounts for bulk purchase for sales promotions, premiums, fund-raising, or educational use. Special editions or book excerpts can also be created to specifications. For details, contact the Special Sales Manager at Human Kinetics.

Printed in the United States of America 10 9 8 7 6 5 4 3

Human Kinetics
Web site: www.HumanKinetics.com

United States: Human Kinetics, P.O. Box 5076, Champaign, IL 61825-5076
800-747-4457
e-mail: humank@hkusa.com

Canada: Human Kinetics, 475 Devonshire Road, Unit 100, Windsor, ON N8Y 2L5
800-465-7301 (in Canada only)
e-mail: orders@hkcanada.com

Europe: Human Kinetics, 107 Bradford Road, Stanningley
Leeds LS28 6AT, United Kingdom
+44 (0) 113 255 5665
e-mail: hk@hkeurope.com

Australia: Human Kinetics, 57A Price Avenue, Lower Mitcham, South Australia 5062
08 8277 1555
e-mail: liaw@hkaustralia.com

New Zealand: Human Kinetics, Division of Sports Distributors NZ Ltd.
P.O. Box 300 226 Albany, North Shore City, Auckland
0064 9 448 1207
e-mail: blairc@hknewz.com

Coaching Youth Soccer

Contents

Welcome to Coaching!

Coaching young people is an exciting way to be involved in sport. But it isn't easy. Some coaches are overwhelmed by the responsibilities involved in helping athletes through their early sport experiences. And that's not surprising, because coaching youngsters requires more than bringing the soccer balls to the field and letting the children play. It involves preparing them physically and mentally to compete effectively, fairly, and safely in their sport, and providing them with a positive role model.

This book will help you meet the challenges *and* experience the many rewards of coaching young athletes. In this book you'll learn how to meet your responsibilities as a coach, communicate well and provide for safety, use a highly effective method—the games approach—to teaching tactics and skills, and learn strategies for coaching on game day. We also provide three sets of season plans to guide you throughout your season.

This book serves as a text for ASEP's Coaching Youth Sport course. If you would like more information about this course or other ASEP courses and resources, please contact us at

ASEP
P.O. Box 5076
Champaign, IL 61825-5076
1-800-747-5698

www.asep.com

Key to Diagrams

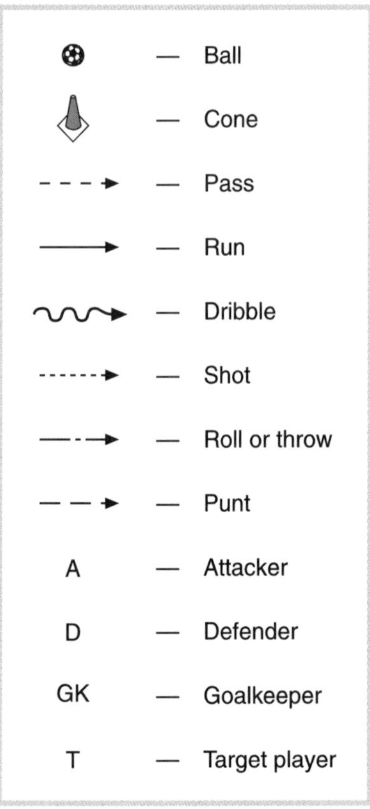

chapter 1

Stepping Into Coaching

If you are like most youth league coaches, you have probably been recruited from the ranks of concerned parents, sport enthusiasts, or community volunteers. Like many rookie and veteran coaches, you probably have had little formal instruction on how to coach. But when the call went out for coaches to assist with the local youth soccer program, you answered because you like children and enjoy soccer, and perhaps because you wanted to be involved in a worthwhile community activity.

Your initial coaching assignment may be difficult. Like many volunteers, you may not know everything there is to know about soccer or about how to work with children. *Coaching Youth Soccer* will help you learn the basics of coaching soccer effectively.

To start, let's take a look at what's involved in being a coach. What are your responsibilities? We'll also talk about how to handle the situation when your child is on the team you coach, and we'll examine five tools for being an effective coach.

Your Responsibilities As a Coach

As a soccer coach, you'll be called upon to do the following:

1. **Provide a safe physical environment.** Playing soccer holds an inherent risk, but as a coach you're responsible for regularly inspecting the practice and competition fields (see the checklists for field surface, outside playing area, and equipment in chapter 6).

2. **Communicate in a positive way.** You'll communicate not only with your players but also with parents, officials, and administrators. Communicate in a way that is positive and that demonstrates you have the best interests of the players at heart. Chapter 2 will help you communicate effectively and positively.

3. **Teach the tactics and skills of soccer.** We'll show you an innovative "games approach" to teaching and practicing the tactics and skills young athletes need to know—an approach that kids thoroughly enjoy. We ask you to help all players be the best they can be. In chapter 5 we'll show you how to teach soccer skills, and in chapter 9 we'll provide season plans for 8- to 9-year-olds, 10- to 11-year-olds, and 12- to 14-year-olds, respectively. In chapter 8 we'll provide descriptions of all the skills you'll need to teach and help you detect and correct errors that players typically make.

4. **Teach the rules of soccer.** We'll ask you to teach your players the rules of soccer. You'll find the main rules in chapter 7.

5. **Direct players in competition.** This includes determining starting lineups and a substitution plan, relating appropriately to officials and to opposing coaches and players, and making tactical decisions during games (see chapter 6). Remember that the focus is not on winning at all costs, but in coaching your kids to compete well, do their best, and strive to win within the rules.

6. **Help your players become fit and value fitness for a lifetime.** We want you to help your players be fit so they can play soccer safely and successfully. We also want your players to learn to become fit on their own, understand the value of fitness, and enjoy training. Thus, we ask you not to make them do push-ups or run laps for punishment. Make it fun to get fit for soccer, and make it fun to play soccer so they'll stay fit for a lifetime.

These are your responsibilities as a coach. But coaching becomes even more complicated when your child is a player on the team you coach. If this is the case, you'll have to take into account your roles as both a coach and a parent, and think about how those roles relate to each other.

Coaching Your Own Child

Many coaches are parents, but the two roles should not be confused. Unlike your role as a parent, as a coach you are responsible not only to yourself and your child, but also to the organization, all the players on the team (including your child), and their parents. Because of this additional responsibility, your behavior on the soccer field will be different from your behavior at home, and your son or daughter may not understand why.

For example, imagine the confusion of a young boy who is the center of his parents' attention at home but is barely noticed by his father/coach in the sport setting. Or consider the mixed signals received by a young girl whose soccer skill is constantly evaluated by a mother/coach who otherwise rarely comments on her daughter's activities. You need to explain to your son or daughter your new responsibilities and how they will affect your relationship when coaching.

Take the following steps to avoid problems in coaching your child:

- Ask your child if he or she wants you to coach the team.
- Explain why you wish to be involved with the team.
- Discuss with your child how your interactions will change when you take on the role of coach at practices or games.
- Limit your coaching behavior to when you are in the coaching role.
- Avoid parenting during practice or game situations, to keep your role clear in your child's mind.
- Reaffirm your love for your child, irrespective of his or her performance on the soccer field.

Now let's look at some of the qualities that will help you become an effective coach.

Five Tools of an Effective Coach

Have you purchased the traditional coaching tools—things like whistles, coaching clothes, sport shoes, and a clipboard? They'll help you coach, but to be a successful coach you'll need five other tools that cannot be bought. These tools are available only through self-examination and hard work; they're easy to remember with the acronym COACH:

C – Comprehension
O – Outlook
A – Affection
C – Character
H – Humor

Comprehension

Comprehension of the rules, tactics, and skills of soccer is required. You must understand the basic elements of the sport. To assist you in learning about the game, we describe rules, tactics, and skills in chapters 7 and 8. We also provide season plans in chapter 9.

To improve your comprehension of soccer, take the following steps:

- Read the sport-specific section of this book in chapters 7, 8, and 9.
- Consider reading other soccer coaching books, including those available from the American Sport Education Program (ASEP).
- Contact youth soccer organizations.
- Attend soccer clinics.
- Talk with more experienced coaches.
- Observe local college, high school, and youth soccer games.
- Watch soccer games on television.

In addition to having soccer knowledge, you must implement proper training and safety methods so your players can participate with little risk of injury. Even then, injuries may occur. And more often than not, you'll be the first person responding to your players' injuries, so be sure you understand the basic emergency care procedures described in chapter 3. Also, read in that chapter how to handle more serious sport injury situations.

Outlook

This coaching tool refers to your perspective and goals—what you are seeking as a coach. The most common coaching objectives are to (a) have fun; (b) help players develop their physical, mental, and social skills;

and (c) win. Thus your *outlook* involves the priorities you set, your planning, and your vision for the future.

While all coaches focus on competition, we want you to focus on *positive* competition, keeping the pursuit of victory in perspective by making decisions that first are in the best interest of the players, and second will help to win the game.

So how do you know if your outlook and priorities are in order? Here's a little test for you:

Which situation would you be most proud of?

a. Knowing that each participant enjoyed playing soccer.

b. Seeing that all players improved their soccer skills.

c. Winning the league championship.

Which statement best reflects your thoughts about sport?

a. If it isn't fun, don't do it.

b. Everyone should learn something every day.

c. Sport isn't fun if you don't win.

How would you like your players to remember you?

a. As a coach who was fun to play for.

b. As a coach who provided a good base of fundamental skills.

c. As a coach who had a winning record.

Which would you most like to hear a parent of a player on your team say?

a. Mike really had a good time playing soccer this year.

b. Nicole learned some important lessons playing soccer this year.

c. Willie played on the first-place soccer team this year.

Which of the following would be the most rewarding moment of your season?

a. Having your team not want to stop playing, even after practice is over.

b. Seeing one of your players finally master the skill of dribbling without constantly looking at the ball.

c. Winning the league championship.

Look over your answers. If you most often selected "a" responses, then having fun is most important to you. A majority of "b" answers suggests that skill development is what attracts you to coaching. And if "c" was your most frequent response, winning is tops on your list of coaching priorities. If your priorities are in order, your players' well-being will take precedence over your team's win-loss record every time.

The American Sport Education Program (ASEP) has a motto that will help you keep your outlook in line with the best interests of the kids on your team. It summarizes in four words all you need to remember when establishing your coaching priorities:

Athletes First, Winning Second

This motto recognizes that striving to win is an important, even vital, part of sports. But it emphatically states that no efforts in striving to win should be made at the expense of the athletes' well-being, development, and enjoyment.

Take the following actions to better define your outlook:

1. Determine your priorities for the season.
2. Prepare for situations that challenge your priorities.
3. Set goals for yourself and your players that are consistent with those priorities.
4. Plan how you and your players can best attain those goals.
5. Review your goals frequently to be sure that you are staying on track.

Affection

This is another vital tool you will want to have in your coaching kit: a genuine concern for the young people you coach. It involves having a love for kids, a desire to share with them your love and knowledge of soccer, and the patience and understanding that allow each individual playing for you to grow from his or her involvement in sport.

You can demonstrate your affection and patience in many ways, including these:

- Make an effort to get to know each player on your team.
- Treat each player as an individual.
- Empathize with players trying to learn new and difficult skills.
- Treat players as you would like to be treated under similar circumstances.
- Be in control of your emotions.
- Show your enthusiasm for being involved with your team.
- Keep an upbeat and positive tone in all of your communications.

Character

The fact that you have decided to coach young soccer players probably means that you think participation in sport is important. But whether or not that participation develops character in your players depends as much on you as it does on the sport itself. How can you build character in your players?

Having good character means modeling appropriate behaviors for sport and life. That means more than just saying the right things. What you say and what you do must match. There is no place in coaching for the "Do as I say, not as I do" philosophy. Challenge, support, encourage, and reward every youngster, and your players will be more likely to accept, even celebrate, their differences. Be in control before, during, and after all practices and contests. And don't be afraid to admit that you were wrong. No one is perfect!

Consider the following steps to being a good role model:

- Take stock of your strengths and weaknesses.
- Build on your strengths.
- Set goals for yourself to improve on those areas you would not like to see copied.
- If you slip up, apologize to your team and to yourself. You'll do better next time.

Humor

Humor is an often-overlooked coaching tool. For our use it means having the ability to laugh at yourself and with your players during practices and contests. Nothing helps balance the tone of a serious skill-learning session like a chuckle or two. And a sense of humor puts in perspective the many mistakes your players will make. So don't get upset over each miscue or respond negatively to erring players. Allow your players and yourself to enjoy the ups, and don't dwell on the downs.

Here are some tips for injecting humor into your practices:

- Make practices fun by including a variety of activities.
- Keep all players involved in games and skill practices.
- Consider laughter by your players a sign of enjoyment, not of waning discipline.
- Smile!

chapter 2

Communicating As a Coach

In chapter 1 you learned about the tools needed to COACH: Comprehension, Outlook, Affection, Character, and Humor. These are essentials for effective coaching; without them, you'd have a difficult time getting started. But none of the tools will work if you don't know how to use them with your athletes—and this requires skillful communication. This chapter examines what communication is and how you can become a more effective communicator-coach.

What's Involved in Communication?

Coaches often mistakenly believe that communication involves only instructing players to do something, but verbal commands are only a small part of the communication process. More than half of what is communicated is nonverbal. So remember when you are coaching: Actions speak louder than words.

Communication in its simplest form involves two people: a sender and a receiver. The sender transmits the message verbally, through facial expressions, and possibly through body language. Once the message is sent, the receiver must assimilate it successfully. A receiver who fails to attend or listen will miss part, if not all, of the message.

How Can I Send More Effective Messages?

Young athletes often have little understanding of the rules and skills of soccer and probably even less confidence in playing it. So they need accurate, understandable, and supportive messages to help them along. That's why your verbal and nonverbal messages are so important.

Verbal Messages

"Sticks and stones may break my bones, but words will never hurt me" isn't true. Spoken words can have a strong and long-lasting effect. And coaches' words are particularly influential because youngsters place great importance on what coaches say. Perhaps you, like many former youth sport participants, have a difficult time remembering much of anything you were told by your elementary school teachers, but you can still recall several specific things your coaches at that level said to you. Such is the lasting effect of a coach's comments to a player.

Whether you are correcting misbehavior, teaching a player how to kick the ball, or praising a player for good effort, you should consider a number of things when sending a message verbally. They include the following:

- Be positive and honest.
- State it clearly and simply.
- Say it loud enough, and say it again.
- Be consistent.

Be Positive and Honest

Nothing turns people off like hearing someone nag all the time, and athletes react similarly to a coach who gripes constantly. Kids particularly need encouragement because they often doubt their ability to perform in a sport. So look for and tell your players what they did well.

But don't cover up poor or incorrect play with rosy words of praise. Kids know all too well when they've erred, and no cheerfully expressed cliché can undo their mistakes. If you fail to acknowledge players' errors, your athletes will think you are a phony.

A good way to correct a performance error is to first point out what the athlete did correctly. Then explain in a positive way what he or she is doing wrong and show him or her how to correct it. Finish by encouraging the athlete and emphasizing the correct performance.

Be sure not to follow a positive statement with the word *but*. For example, don't say, "That was good location on your pass, Kelly. But if you follow through with your kick a little more, you'll get a little more zip on the ball." Saying it this way causes many kids to ignore the positive statement and focus on the negative one. Instead, say something like "That was good location on your pass, Kelly. And if you follow through with your kick a little more, you'll get a little more zip on the ball. That was right on target. That's the way to go."

State It Clearly and Simply

Positive and honest messages are good, but only if expressed directly in words your players understand. "Beating around the bush" is ineffective and inefficient. And if you do ramble, your players will miss the point of your message and probably lose interest. Here are some tips for saying things clearly:

- Organize your thoughts before speaking to your athletes.
- Explain things thoroughly, but don't bore them with long-winded monologues.
- Use language your players can understand. However, avoid trying to be hip by using their age group's slang.

Say It Loud Enough, and Say It Again

Talk to your team in a voice that all members can hear and interpret. A crisp, vigorous voice commands attention and respect; garbled and weak speech is tuned out. It's OK—in fact, appropriate—to soften your voice when speaking to a player individually about a personal problem. But most of the time your messages will be for all your players to hear, so make sure they can! An enthusiastic voice also motivates players and tells them you enjoy being their coach. A word of caution, however: Don't dominate the setting with a booming voice that distracts attention from players' performances.

Sometimes what you say, even if stated loudly and clearly, won't sink in the first time. This may be particularly true when young athletes hear words they don't understand. To avoid boring repetition and yet still get your message across, say the same thing in a slightly different way. For instance, you might first tell your players, "Mark your opponents tighter!" If they don't appear to understand, you might say, "When your opponents are in scoring range, you can't give them the chance to shoot or pass the ball forward." The second form of the message may get through to players who missed it the first time around.

Be Consistent

People often say things in ways that imply a different message. For example, a touch of sarcasm added to the words "Way to go!" sends an entirely different message than the words themselves suggest. Avoid sending such mixed messages. Keep the tone of your voice consistent with the words you use. And don't say something one day and contradict it the next; players will get their wires crossed.

Nonverbal Messages

Just as you should be consistent in the tone of voice and words you use, you should also keep your verbal and nonverbal messages consistent. An extreme example of failing to do this would be shaking your head, indicating disapproval, while at the same time telling a player "Nice try." Which is the player to believe, your gesture or your words?

Messages can be sent nonverbally in a number of ways. Facial expressions and body language are just two of the more obvious forms of nonverbal signals that can help you when you coach.

Facial Expressions

The look on a person's face is the quickest clue to what he or she thinks or feels. Your players know this, so they will study your face, looking for any sign that will tell them more than the words you say. Don't try to fool them by putting on a happy or blank "mask." They'll see through it, and you'll lose credibility.

Serious, stone-faced expressions are no help to kids who need cues as to how they are performing. They will just assume you're unhappy or disinterested. Don't be afraid to smile. A smile from a coach can give a great boost to an unsure athlete. Plus, a smile lets your players know that you are happy coaching them. But don't overdo it, or your players won't be able to tell when you are genuinely pleased by something they've done or when you are just putting on a smiling face.

Body Language

What would your players think you were feeling if you came to practice slouched over, with your head down and shoulders slumped? Tired? Bored? Unhappy? What would they think you were feeling if you watched them during a contest with your hands on your hips, your jaws clenched, and your face reddened? Upset with them? Disgusted at an official? Mad at a fan? Probably some or all of these things would enter your players' minds. And none of these impressions is the kind you want your players to have of you. That's why you should carry yourself in a pleasant, confident, and vigorous manner. Such a posture not only projects happiness with your coaching role but also provides a good example for your young players, who may model your behavior.

Physical contact can also be a very important use of body language. A handshake, a pat on the head, an arm around the shoulder, or even a big hug are effective ways of showing approval, concern, affection, and joy to your players. Youngsters are especially in need of this type of nonverbal message. Keep within the obvious moral and legal limits, of course, but don't be reluctant to touch your players, sending a message that can only truly be expressed in that way.

How Can I Improve My Receiving Skills?

Now, let's examine the other half of the communication process—receiving messages. Too often very good senders are very poor receivers of messages. But as a coach of young athletes, you must be able to fulfill both roles effectively.

The requirements for receiving messages are quite simple, but receiving skills are perhaps less satisfying and therefore underdeveloped compared to sending skills. People seem to naturally enjoy hearing themselves talk more than hearing others talk. But if you read about the keys to receiving messages and make a strong effort to use them with your players, you'll be surprised by what you've been missing.

Attention!

First, you must pay attention; you must want to hear what others have to communicate to you. That's not always easy when you're busy coaching and have many things competing for your attention. But in one-on-one or team meetings with players, you must really focus on what they are telling you, both verbally and nonverbally. You'll be amazed at the little signals you pick up. Not only will such focused attention help you catch every word your players say, but also you'll notice your players' moods and physical states. In addition, you'll get an idea of your players' feelings toward you and other players on the team.

Listen CARE-FULLY

How we receive messages from others, perhaps more than anything else we do, demonstrates how much we care for the sender and what that person has to tell us. If you care little for your players or have little regard for what they have to say, it will show in how you attend and listen to them. Check yourself. Do you find your mind wandering to what you are going to do after practice while one of your players is talking to you? Do you frequently have to ask your players, "What did you say?" If so, you need to work on your receiving mechanics of attending and listening. But perhaps the most critical question you should ask yourself, if you find that you're missing the messages your players send, is this: Do I care?

Providing Feedback

So far we've discussed separately the sending and receiving of messages. But we all know that senders and receivers switch roles several times during an interaction. One person initiates a communication by sending a message to another person, who then receives the message. The receiver then switches roles and becomes the sender by responding to the person who sent the initial message. These verbal and nonverbal responses are called *feedback*.

Your players will be looking to you for feedback all the time. They will want to know how you think they are performing, what you think of their ideas, and whether their efforts please you. Obviously, you can respond in many different ways. How you respond will strongly affect your players. They will respond most favorably to positive feedback.

Praising players when they have performed or behaved well is an effective way of getting them to repeat (or try to repeat) that behavior in the future. And positive feedback for effort is an especially effective way to motivate youngsters to work on difficult skills. So rather than shouting and providing negative feedback to players who have made mistakes, try offering players positive feedback, letting them know what they did correctly and how they can improve.

Sometimes just the way you word feedback can make it more positive than negative. For example, instead of saying, "Don't shoot the ball that way," you might say, "Shoot the ball this way." Then your players will be focusing on what to do instead of what not to do.

You can give positive feedback verbally and nonverbally. Telling a player, especially in front of teammates, that he or she has performed well is a great way to boost the confidence of a youngster. And a pat on the back or a handshake can be a very tangible way of communicating your recognition of a player's performance.

Who Else Do I Need to Communicate With?

Coaching involves not only sending and receiving messages and providing proper feedback to players, but also interacting with parents, fans, game officials, and opposing coaches. If you don't communicate effectively with these groups of people, your coaching career will be unpleasant and short-lived. So try the following suggestions for communicating with these groups.

Parents

A player's parents need to be assured that their son or daughter is under the direction of a coach who is both knowledgeable about the sport and concerned about the youngster's well-being. You can put their worries to rest by holding a preseason parent-orientation meeting in which you describe your background and your approach to coaching.

If parents contact you with a concern during the season, listen to them closely and try to offer positive responses. If you need to communicate with parents, catch them after a practice, give them a phone call, or send a note through the mail. Messages sent to parents through players are too often lost, misinterpreted, or forgotten.

Fans

The stands probably won't be overflowing at your contests, but that only means that you'll more easily hear the few fans who criticize your coaching. When you hear something negative said about the job you're doing, don't respond. Keep calm, consider whether the message had any value, and if not, forget it. Acknowledging critical, unwarranted comments from a fan during a contest will only encourage others to voice their opinions. So put away your "rabbit ears" and communicate to fans, through your actions, that you are a confident, competent coach.

Prepare your players for fans' criticisms. Tell them it is you, not the spectators, they should listen to. If you notice that one of your players is rattled by a fan's comment, reassure the player that your evaluation is more objective and favorable—and is the one that counts.

Contest Officials

How you communicate with officials will have a great influence on the way your players behave toward them. Therefore, you need to set an example. Greet officials with a handshake, an introduction, and perhaps some casual conversation about the upcoming contest. Indicate your respect for them before, during, and after the contest. Don't make nasty remarks, shout, or use disrespectful body gestures. Your players will see you do it, and they'll get the idea that such behavior is appropriate. Plus, if the official hears or sees you, the communication between the two of you will break down.

Opposing Coaches

Make an effort to visit with the coach of the opposing team before the game. During the game, don't get into a personal feud with the opposing coach. Remember, it's the kids, not the coaches, who are competing. And by getting along well with the opposing coach, you'll show your players that competition involves cooperation.

chapter 3

Providing for Players' Safety

One of your players appears to break free down the field, dribbling the ball. But a defender catches up with, and accidentally trips, the goal-bound player. You notice that your player is not getting up from the ground and seems to be in pain. What do you do?

No coach wants to see players get hurt. But injury remains a reality of sport participation; consequently, you must be prepared to provide first aid when injuries occur and to protect yourself against unjustified lawsuits. Fortunately, there are many preventive measures coaches can institute to reduce the risk. In this chapter we describe

- steps you can take to prevent injuries,
- first aid and emergency responses for when injuries occur, and
- your legal responsibilities as a coach.

The Game Plan for Safety

You can't prevent all injuries from happening, but you can take preventive measures that give your players the best possible chance for injury-free participation. In creating the safest possible environment for your athletes, we'll explore what you can do in these six areas:

- Preseason physical examinations
- Physical conditioning
- Equipment and facilities inspection
- Matching athletes and inherent risks
- Proper supervision and record keeping
- Environmental conditions

We'll begin with what should take place *before* the season begins: the preseason physical examination.

Preseason Physical Examination

We recommend that your players have a physical examination before participating in soccer. The exam should address the most likely areas of medical concern and identify youngsters at high risk. We also suggest that you have players' parents or guardians sign a participation agreement form and a release form to allow their children to be treated in case of an emergency.

Physical Conditioning

Players need to be in, or get in, shape to play the game at the level expected. To do so, they'll need to have adequate *cardiorespiratory fitness* and *muscular fitness.*

Cardiorespiratory fitness involves the body's ability to store and use oxygen and fuels efficiently to power muscle contractions. As players get in better shape, their bodies are able to more efficiently deliver oxygen and fuels to muscles and carry off carbon dioxides and other wastes. Soccer involves lots of running; most players will be moving nearly continuously and making short bursts throughout a game. Youngsters who aren't as fit as their peers often overextend in trying to make up for their lack of fitness, which could result in lightheadedness and nausea.

An advantage of teaching soccer with the games approach is that kids are active during almost the entire practice; there is no standing around in lines, watching teammates take part in drills. Players will be attaining higher levels of cardiorespiratory fitness as the season progresses simply by taking part in practice. However, watch closely for signs of low levels of cardiorespiratory fitness; don't let your athletes do too much until they're fit. You might privately counsel youngsters who appear overly winded, suggesting that they train outside of practice to increase their fitness.

Muscular fitness encompasses strength, muscle endurance, power, speed, and flexibility. This type of fitness is affected by physical maturity, as well as by strength training and other types of training. Your players will likely exhibit a relatively wide range of muscular fitness. Those who have greater muscular fitness will be able to run faster and kick harder. They will also sustain fewer muscular injuries, and any injuries that do occur will tend to be more minor in nature. And in case of injury, recovery rate is accelerated in those with higher levels of muscular fitness.

Two other components of fitness and injury prevention are the warm-up and the cool-down. Although young bodies are generally very limber, they, too, can get tight from inactivity. The warm-up should address each muscle group and get the heart rate elevated in preparation for strenuous activity. Have players warm up for 5 to 10 minutes by playing easy games and stretching.

As practice winds down, slow players' heart rates with an easy jog or walk. Then have players stretch for five minutes to help avoid stiff muscles and make them less tight before the next practice or contest.

Equipment and Facilities Inspection

Another way to prevent injuries is to ensure that all players have adequate shin guards and that they wear them. Remember also to examine regularly the field on which your players practice and play. Remove hazards, report conditions you cannot remedy, and request maintenance as necessary. If unsafe conditions exist, either make adaptations to avoid risk to your players' safety or stop the practice or game until safe conditions have been restored.

Player Match-Ups and Inherent Risks

We recommend you group teams in two-year age ranges if possible. You'll encounter fewer mismatches in physical maturation with narrow age ranges. Even so, two 12-year-old boys might differ by 90 pounds in weight, a foot in height, and three or four years in emotional and intellectual maturity. This presents dangers for the less mature. Whenever possible, match players against opponents of similar size and physical maturity. Such an approach gives smaller, less mature youngsters a better chance to succeed and avoid injury while providing more mature players with a greater challenge. Closely supervise games so that the more mature do not put the less mature at undue risk.

Proper matching helps protect you from certain liability concerns. But you must also warn players of the inherent risks involved in playing soccer, because "failure to warn" is one of the most successful arguments in lawsuits against coaches. So, thoroughly explain the inherent risks of soccer, and make sure each player knows, understands, and appreciates those risks.

The preseason parent-orientation meeting is a good opportunity to explain the risks of the sport to both parents and players. It is also a good occasion on which to have both the players and their parents sign waivers releasing you from liability should an injury occur. Such waivers do not relieve you of responsibility for your players' well-being, but they are recommended by lawyers.

Proper Supervision and Record Keeping

To ensure players' safety, you will need to provide both general supervision and specific supervision. *General supervision* is being in the area of activity so that you can see and hear what is happening. You should be

- immediately accessible to the activity and able to oversee the entire activity,
- alert to conditions that may be dangerous to players and ready to take action to protect them, and
- able to react immediately and appropriately to emergencies.

Specific supervision is direct supervision of an activity at practice. For example, you should provide specific supervision when you teach new skills and continue it until your athletes understand the requirements of the activity, the risks involved, and their own ability to perform in light of these risks. You need to also provide specific supervision when you notice either players breaking rules or a change in the condition of your athletes.

As a general rule, the more dangerous the activity, the more specific the supervision required. This suggests that more specific supervision is required with younger and less experienced athletes.

As part of your supervision duty, you are expected to foresee potentially dangerous situations and to be positioned to help prevent them from occurring. This requires that you know soccer well, especially the rules that are intended to provide for safety. Prohibit dangerous horseplay, and hold practices only under safe weather conditions. These specific supervisory activities, applied consistently, will make the play environment safer for your players and will help protect you from liability if a mishap does occur.

For further protection, keep records of your season plans, practice plans, and players' injuries. Season and practice plans come in handy when you need evidence that players have been taught certain skills, whereas accurate, detailed injury report forms offer protection against unfounded lawsuits. Ask for these forms from your sponsoring organization (appendix A has a sample injury report form), and hold onto these records for several years so that an "old soccer injury" of a former player doesn't come back to haunt you.

Environmental Conditions

Most problems caused by environmental factors are related to excessive heat or cold, though you should also consider other environmental factors such as severe weather and pollution. A little thought about the potential problems and a little effort to ensure adequate protection for your athletes will prevent most serious emergencies that are related to environmental conditions.

Heat

On hot, humid days the body has difficulty cooling itself. Because the air is already saturated with water vapor (humidity), sweat doesn't evaporate as easily. Therefore, body sweat is a less effective cooling agent, and the body retains extra heat. Hot, humid environments make athletes prone to heat exhaustion and heatstroke (see more on these in "Serious Injuries" on pages 29-31). And if *you* think it's hot or humid, it's worse on the kids—not only because they're more active, but also because youngsters under the age of 12 have a more difficult time than adults regulating their body temperatures. To provide for players' safety in hot or humid conditions, take the following preventive measures.

◎ **Monitor weather conditions and adjust practices accordingly.** Figure 3.1 shows the specific air temperatures and humidity percentages that can be hazardous.

◎ **Acclimatize players to exercising in high heat and humidity.** Athletes can make adjustments to high heat and humidity over 7 to 10 days. During this time, hold practices at low to moderate activity levels and give the players water breaks every 20 minutes.

◎ **Switch to light clothing.** Players should wear shorts and white T-shirts.

◎ **Identify and monitor players who are prone to heat illness.** Players who are overweight, heavily muscled, or out of shape will be more prone to heat illness, as are athletes who work excessively hard or who have suffered heat illness before. Closely monitor these athletes and give them water breaks every 15 to 20 minutes.

◎ **Make sure athletes replace water lost through sweat.** Encourage your players to drink one liter of water each day outside of practice and contest times, to drink eight ounces of water every 20 minutes during practice or competition, and to drink four to eight ounces of water 20 minutes before practice or competition.

◎ **Replenish electrolytes lost through sweat.** Sodium (salt) and potassium are lost through sweat. The best way to replace these nutrients is by eating a normal diet that contains fresh fruits and vegetables. Bananas are a good source of potassium. The normal American diet contains plenty of salt, so players don't need to go overboard in salting their food to replace lost sodium.

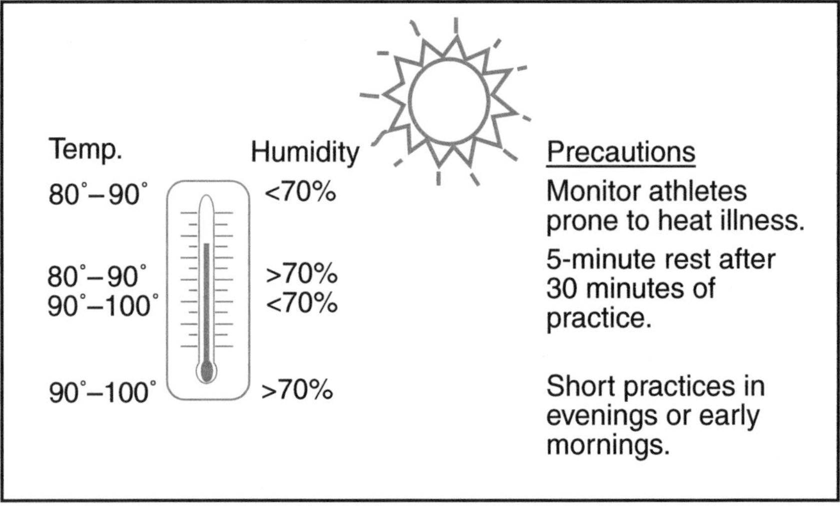

Figure 3.1 Warm-weather precautions.

Water, Water Everywhere

Encourage players to drink plenty of water before, during, and after practice. Because water makes up 45 percent to 65 percent of a youngster's body weight and water weighs about a pound per pint, the loss of even a little bit of water can have severe consequences for the body's systems. And it doesn't have to be hot and humid for players to become dehydrated. Nor do players have to feel thirsty; in fact, by the time they are aware of their thirst, they are long overdue for a drink.

Cold

When a person is exposed to cold weather, the body temperature starts to drop below normal. To counteract this, the body shivers and reduces the blood flow to gain or conserve heat. But no matter how effective the body's natural heating mechanism is, the body will better withstand cold temperatures if it is prepared to handle them. To reduce the risk of cold-related illnesses, make sure players wear appropriate protective clothing, and keep them active to maintain body heat. Also monitor the windchill (see figure 3.2).

Severe Weather

Severe weather refers to a host of potential dangers, including lightning storms, tornadoes, hail, and heavy rains (which can cause injuries by creating sloppy field conditions).

Temperature (˚F)

Wind speed (mph)	0	5	10	15	20	25	30	35	40
40	-55	-45	-35	-30	-20	-15	-5	0	10
35	-50	-40	-35	-30	-20	-10	-5	5	10
30	-50	-40	-30	-25	-20	-10	0	5	10
25	-45	-35	-30	-20	-15	-5	0	10	15
20	-35	-30	-25	-15	-10	0	5	10	20
15	-30	-25	-20	-10	-5	0	10	15	25
10	-20	-15	-10	0	5	10	15	20	30
5	-5	0	5	10	15	20	25	30	35

Flesh may freeze within 1 minute (shaded cells)

Windchill temperature (˚F)

Figure 3.2 Windchill factor index.

Lightning is of special concern because it can come up quickly and can cause great harm or even kill. For each 5-second count from the flash of lightning to the bang of thunder, lightning is one mile away. A flash-bang of 10 seconds means lightning is two miles away; a flash-bang of 15 seconds indicates lightning is three miles away. A practice or competition should be stopped for the day if lightning is three miles away or less (15 seconds or less from flash to bang).

Safe places in which to take cover when lightning strikes are fully enclosed metal vehicles with the windows up, enclosed buildings, and low ground (under cover of bushes, if possible). It's *not* safe to be near metallic objects—flagpoles, fences, light poles, metal bleachers, and so on. Also avoid trees, water, and open fields.

Cancel practice when under either a tornado watch or warning. If for some reason you are practicing or competing when a tornado is nearby, you should get inside a building if possible. If not, lie in a ditch or other low-lying area or crouch near a strong building, and use your arms to protect your head and neck.

The keys to handling severe weather are caution and prudence. Don't try to get that last 10 minutes of practice in if lightning is on the horizon. Don't continue to play in heavy rains. Many storms can strike both quickly and ferociously. Respect the weather and play it safe.

Air Pollution

Poor air quality and smog can present real dangers to your players. Both short- and long-term lung damage are possible from participating in unsafe air. Although it's true that participating in clean air is not possible in many areas, restricting activity is recommended when the air-quality ratings are worse than moderate or when there is a smog alert. Your local health department or air-quality control board can inform you of the air-quality ratings for your area and when restricting activities is recommended.

Responding to Players' Injuries

No matter how good and thorough your prevention program is, injuries may occur. When injury does strike, chances are you will be the one in charge. The severity and nature of the injury will determine how actively involved you'll be in treating the injury. But regardless of how seriously a player is hurt, it is your responsibility to know what steps to take. So let's look at how you should prepare to provide basic emergency care to your injured athletes and take the appropriate action when an injury does occur.

Being Prepared

Being prepared to provide basic emergency care involves three steps: being trained in cardiopulmonary resuscitation (CPR) and first aid, having an appropriately stocked first aid kit on hand at practices and games, and having an emergency plan.

CPR and First Aid Training

We recommend that all coaches receive CPR and first aid training from a nationally recognized organization (the National Safety Council, the American Heart Association, the American Red Cross, or the American Sport Education Program). You should be certified based on a practical test and a written test of knowledge. CPR training should include pediatric and adult basic life support and obstructed airway procedures.

First Aid Kit

A well-stocked first aid kit should include the following:

- List of emergency phone numbers
- Change for a pay phone (or cell phone and batteries)
- Face shield (for rescue breathing and CPR)
- Bandage scissors
- Plastic bags for crushed ice
- 3-inch and 4-inch elastic wraps
- Triangular bandages
- Sterile gauze pads—3-inch and 4-inch squares
- Saline solution for eyes
- Contact lens case
- Mirror
- Penlight
- Tongue depressors
- Cotton swabs
- Butterfly strips
- Bandage strips—assorted sizes
- Alcohol or peroxide
- Antibacterial soap
- First aid cream or antibacterial ointment
- Petroleum jelly

- Tape adherent and tape remover
- 1 $\frac{1}{2}$-inch white athletic tape
- Prewrap
- Sterile gauze rolls
- Insect sting kit
- Safety pins
- $\frac{1}{8}$-inch, $\frac{1}{4}$-inch, and $\frac{1}{2}$-inch foam rubber
- Disposable surgical gloves
- Thermometer

Emergency Plan

An emergency plan is the final step in preparing to take appropriate action for severe or serious injuries. The plan calls for three steps:

1. **Evaluate the injured player.** Your CPR and first aid training will guide you here.

2. **Call the appropriate medical personnel.** If possible, delegate the responsibility of seeking medical help to another calm and responsible adult who is on hand for all practices and games. Write out a list of emergency phone numbers and keep it with you at practices and games. Include the following phone numbers:

   - Rescue unit
   - Hospital
   - Physician
   - Police
   - Fire department

   Take each athlete's emergency information to every practice and game (see appendix B). This information includes the person to contact in case of an emergency, what types of medications the athlete is using, what types of drugs he or she is allergic to, and so on.

   Give an emergency response card (see appendix C) to the contact person calling for emergency assistance. This provides the information the contact person needs to convey and will help keep the person calm, knowing that everything he or she needs to communicate is on the card. Also complete an injury report form (see appendix A) and keep it on file for any injury that occurs.

3. **Provide first aid.** If medical personnel are not on hand at the time of the injury, you should provide first aid care to the extent of your

qualifications. Again, while your CPR and first aid training will guide you here, the following are important guidelines:

- Do not move the injured athlete if the injury is to the head, neck, or back; if a large joint (ankle, knee, elbow, shoulder) is dislocated; or if the pelvis, a rib, or an arm or leg is fractured.
- Calm the injured athlete and keep others away from him or her as much as possible.
- Evaluate whether the athlete's breathing is stopped or irregular, and if necessary, clear the airway with your fingers.
- Administer artificial respiration if the athlete's breathing has stopped. Administer CPR if the athlete's circulation has stopped.
- Remain with the athlete until medical personnel arrive.

Emergency Steps

Your emergency plan should follow this sequence:

1. Check the athlete's level of consciousness.
2. Have a contact person call the appropriate medical personnel and the athlete's parents.
3. Send someone to wait for the rescue team and direct them to the injured athlete.
4. Assess the injury.
5. Administer first aid.
6. Assist emergency medical personnel in preparing the athlete for transportation to a medical facility.
7. Appoint someone to go with the athlete if the parents are not available. This person should be responsible, calm, and familiar with the athlete. Assistant coaches or parents are best for this job.
8. Complete an injury report form while the incident is fresh in your mind (see appendix A).

Taking Appropriate Action

Proper CPR and first aid training, a well-stocked first aid kit, and an emergency plan help prepare you to take appropriate action when an injury occurs. We spoke in the previous section about the importance of providing first aid *to the extent of your qualifications.* Don't "play doctor" with injuries; sort out minor injuries that you can treat from those for which you need to call for medical assistance.

Next we'll look at taking the appropriate action for minor injuries and more serious injuries.

Minor Injuries

Although no injury seems minor to the person experiencing it, most injuries are neither life-threatening nor severe enough to restrict participation. When such injuries occur, you can take an active role in their initial treatment.

Scrapes and Cuts. When one of your players has an open wound, the first thing you should do is put on a pair of disposable surgical gloves or some other effective blood barrier. Then follow these four steps:

1. *Stop the bleeding* by applying direct pressure with a clean dressing to the wound and elevating it. The player may be able to apply this pressure while you put on your gloves. Do not remove the dressing if it becomes soaked with blood. Instead, place an additional dressing on top of the one already in place. If bleeding continues, elevate the injured area above the heart and maintain pressure.

2. *Cleanse the wound* thoroughly once the bleeding is controlled. A good rinsing with a forceful stream of water, and perhaps light scrubbing with soap, will help prevent infection.

3. *Protect the wound* with sterile gauze or a bandage strip. If the player continues to participate, apply protective padding over the injured area.

4. *Remove and dispose of gloves* carefully to prevent you or anyone else from coming into contact with blood.

For bloody noses not associated with serious facial injury, have the athlete sit and lean slightly forward. Then pinch the player's nostrils shut. If the bleeding continues after several minutes, or if the athlete has a history of nosebleeds, seek medical assistance.

Treating Bloody Injuries

You shouldn't let a fear of acquired immune deficiency syndrome (AIDS) stop you from helping a player. You are only at risk if you allow contaminated blood to come in contact with an open wound, so the surgical disposable gloves that you wear will protect you from AIDS should one of your players carry this disease. Check with your director or your organization for more information about protecting yourself and your participants from AIDS.

Strains and Sprains. The physical demands of soccer practices and games often result in injury to the muscles or tendons (strains) or to the ligaments (sprains). When your players suffer minor strains or sprains, immediately apply the PRICE method of injury care:

P – Protect the athlete and injured body part from further danger or trauma.

R – Rest the area to avoid further damage and foster healing.

I – Ice the area to reduce swelling and pain.

C – Compress the area by securing an ice bag in place with an elastic wrap.

E – Elevate the injury above heart level to keep the blood from pooling in the area.

Bumps and Bruises. Inevitably, soccer players make contact with each other and with the ground. If the force applied to a body part at impact is great enough, a bump or bruise will result. Many players continue playing with such sore spots, but if the bump or bruise is large and painful, you should act appropriately. Use the PRICE method for injury care and monitor the injury. If swelling, discoloration, and pain have lessened, the player may resume participation with protective padding; if not, the player should be examined by a physician.

Serious Injuries

Head, neck, and back injuries; fractures; and injuries that cause a player to lose consciousness are among a class of injuries that you cannot and should not try to treat yourself. In these cases you should follow the emergency plan outlined on pages 26-27. We do want to examine more closely your role, however, in preventing and handling two heat illnesses: heat exhaustion and heatstroke.

Heat Exhaustion. Heat exhaustion is a shocklike condition caused by dehydration and electrolyte depletion. Symptoms include headache, nausea, dizziness, chills, fatigue, and extreme thirst (see figure 3.3 for heat exhaustion and heatstroke symptoms). Profuse sweating is a key sign of heat exhaustion. Other signs include pale, cool, and clammy skin; rapid, weak pulse; loss of coordination; and dilated pupils.

A player suffering from heat exhaustion should rest in a cool, shaded area; drink cool water; and have ice applied to the neck, back, or abdomen to help cool the body. You may have to administer CPR if necessary or send for emergency medical assistance if the athlete doesn't recover or his or her condition worsens. Under no conditions should the athlete return to activity that day or before he or she regains all the weight lost through sweat. If the player has to see a physician, he or she shouldn't return to the team until he or she has a written release from the physician.

Heatstroke. Heatstroke is a life-threatening condition in which the body stops sweating and body temperature rises dangerously high. It occurs when dehydration causes a malfunction in the body's temperature control center in the brain. Symptoms include the feeling of being on fire (extremely hot), nausea, confusion, irritability, and fatigue. Signs include hot, dry, and flushed or red skin (this is a key sign); lack of sweat; rapid pulse; rapid breathing; constricted pupils; vomiting; diarrhea; and possibly seizures, unconsciousness, or respiratory or cardiac arrest. See figure 3.3 for heat exhaustion and heatstroke symptoms.

Send for emergency medical assistance immediately and have the player rest in a cool, shaded area. Remove excess clothing and equipment from the player, and cool the player's body with cool, wet towels

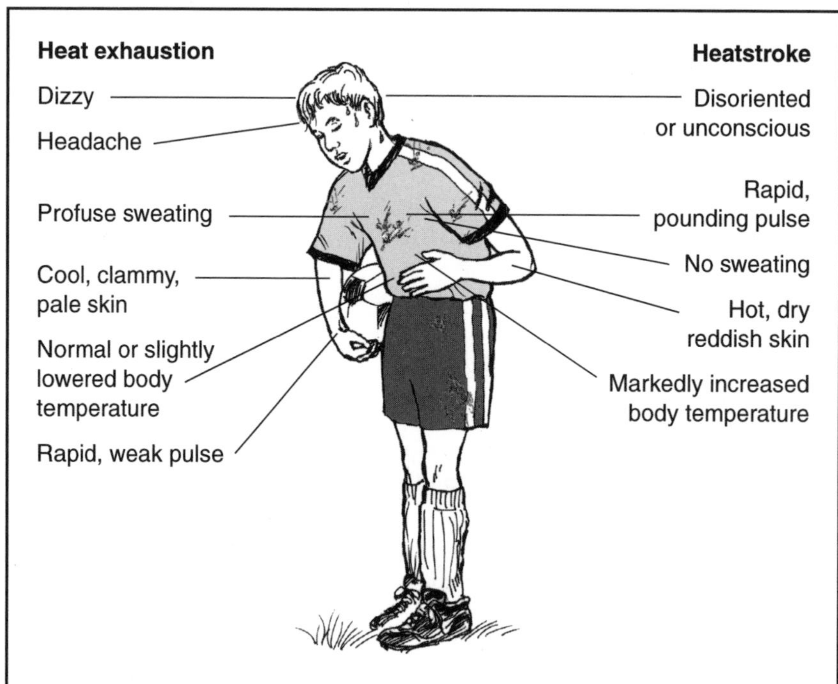

Figure 3.3 Symptoms of heat exhaustion and heatstroke.

or by pouring cool water over him or her. Apply ice packs to the armpits, neck, back, abdomen, and between the legs. If the player is conscious, have him or her drink cool water. If the player is unconscious, place the player on his or her side to allow fluids and vomit to drain from the mouth.

An athlete who has suffered heatstroke may not return to the team until he or she has a written release from a physician.

Protecting Yourself

When one of your players is injured, naturally your first concern is his or her well-being. Your feelings for youngsters, after all, are what made you decide to coach. Unfortunately, there is something else that you must consider: Can you be held liable for the injury?

From a legal standpoint, a coach has nine duties to fulfill. We've discussed all but planning in this chapter. (See chapter 5 for developing practice plans, and chapter 9 for guidance on season planning.) The following is a summary of your legal duties:

1. Provide a safe environment.
2. Properly plan the activity.
3. Provide adequate and proper equipment.
4. Match, or equate, athletes.
5. Warn of inherent risks in the sport.
6. Supervise the activity closely.
7. Evaluate athletes for injury or incapacitation.
8. Know emergency procedures and first aid.
9. Keep adequate records.

Keep records of your season plan and practice plans and of players' injuries. Season and practice plans come in handy when you need evidence that players have been taught certain skills, and injury reports offer protection against unfounded lawsuits. Hold onto these records for several years so that an "old injury" of a former player doesn't come back to haunt you.

In addition to fulfilling these nine legal duties, you should check your organization's insurance coverage and your insurance coverage to make sure these policies will protect you from liability.

chapter 4

The Games Approach to Coaching Soccer

Do you remember how as a kid you were taught by adults to play a sport, either in an organized sport program or physical education class? They probably taught you the basic skills using a series of drills that, if the truth be known, you found very boring. As you began to learn the basic skills, they eventually taught you the tactics of the game, showing you when to use these skills in various game situations. Do you remember how impatient you became during what seemed to be endless instruction, and how much you just wanted to play? Well, forget this traditional approach to teaching sports.

Now can you recall learning a sport by playing with a group of your friends in the neighborhood? You didn't learn the basic skills first; no time for that. You began playing immediately. If you didn't know the basic things to do, your friends told you quickly during the game so they could keep playing. Try to remember, because we're going to ask you to use a very similar approach to teaching soccer to young people called the games approach, an approach we think knocks the socks off the traditional approach.

On the surface, it would seem to make sense to introduce soccer by first teaching the basic skills of the sport and then the tactics of the game, but we've discovered that this approach has disadvantages. First, it teaches the skills of the sport out of the context of the game. Kids may learn to control, kick, pass, dribble, and head the ball, but they find it difficult to use these skills in the real game. This is because they do not yet understand the fundamental tactics of soccer and do not appreciate how best to use their newfound skills.

Second, learning skills by doing drills outside of the context of the game is so-o-o-o boring. The single biggest turnoff about adults teaching kids sports is that we overorganize the instruction and deprive kids of their intrinsic desire to play the game.

As a coach we're asking that you teach soccer the games approach way. Clear the traditional approach out of your mind. Once you fully understand the games approach, you'll quickly see its superiority in teaching soccer. Not only will kids learn the game better, but you and your players will have much more fun. And as a bonus, you'll have far fewer discipline problems.

With the games approach to teaching soccer, we begin with a game. This will be a modified and much smaller game designed to suit the age and ability of the players. As the kids play in these "mini" games, you can begin to help them understand the nature of the game and to appreciate simple concepts of positioning and tactics. When your players understand what they must do in the game, they are then eager to develop the skills to play it. Now motivated to learn the skills, you can demonstrate the skills of the game, practice using game-like drills, and provide individual instruction by identifying players' errors and helping to correct them.

In the traditional approach to teaching sports, players do this:

Learn the skill → Learn the tactics → Play the game

In the games approach players do this:

Play the game → Learn the tactics → Learn the skill

In the past we have placed too much emphasis on the learning of skills and not enough on learning how to play skillfully—that is, how to use those skills in competition. The games approach, in contrast, emphasizes learning what to do first, then how to do it. Moreover—and this is a really important point—the games approach lets kids discover what to do in the game not by your telling them, but by their experiencing it. What you do as an effective coach is help them discover what they've experienced.

In contrast to the "skill-drill-kill the enthusiasm" approach, the games approach is a guided discovery method of teaching. It empowers your kids to solve the problems that arise in the game, and that's a big part of the fun in learning a game.

Now let's look more closely at the games approach to see the four-step process for teaching soccer:

1. Play a modified soccer game.
2. Help the players discover what they need to do to play the game successfully.
3. Teach the skills of the game.
4. Practice the skills in another game.

Step 1. Play a Modified Soccer Game

Okay, it's the first day of practice; some of the kids are eager to get started, while others are obviously apprehensive. Some have rarely kicked a ball, most don't know the rules, and none knows the positions in soccer. What do you do?

If you use the traditional approach, you start with a little warm-up activity, then line the players up for a simple kicking drill and go from there. With the games approach, you begin by playing a modified game that is developmentally appropriate for the level of the players and also designed to focus on learning a specific part of the game.

Modifying the game emphasizes a limited number of situations in the game. This is one way you "guide" your players to discover certain tactics in the game.

For instance, you have your players play a 2 v 2 (two players versus two players) game in a 20- by 20-yard playing area. The objective of the game is to make four passes before attempting to score. Playing the game this way forces players to think about what they have to do to keep possession of the ball.

Step 2. Help the Players Discover What They Need to Do

As your players are playing the game, look for the right spot to "freeze" the action, step in, and hold a brief question-and-answer session to discuss problems they were having in carrying out the goals of the game. You don't need to pop in on the first miscue, but if they repeat the same types of mental or physical mistakes a few times in a row, step in and ask them questions that relate to the aim of the game and the necessary skills required. The best time to interrupt the game is when you notice that they are having trouble carrying out the main goal, or aim, of the game. By stopping the game, freezing action, and asking questions, you'll help them understand

- what the aim of the game is,
- what they must do to achieve that aim, and
- what skills they must use to achieve that aim.

For example, your players just played a game in which the objective is to make four passes before attempting to score, but they are having trouble doing so. Interrupt the action and ask the following questions:

Coach: What are you supposed to do in this game?

Players: Pass the ball four times before scoring.

Coach: What does your team have to do to keep the ball for four passes in a row?

Players: Pass the ball.

Coach: Yes, and what else?

Players: You have to be able to get the pass, too.

Coach: OK. You have to be able to pass the ball and get the ball when it's passed. Why don't we practice passing the ball and getting the pass?

Through the modified game and skillful questioning on your part, your players realize that accurate passing and receiving skills are essential to their success in controlling the ball. Just as important, rather than *telling* them that passing and receiving skills are critical, you led them to that discovery through a well-designed modified game and through questions. This questioning that leads to players' discovery is a crucial part of the games approach. Essentially you'll be asking your players—usually literally—"What do you need to do to succeed in this situation?"

Asking the right questions is a very important part of your teaching. At first asking questions will be difficult because your players have little or no experience with the game. And if you've learned sport through the traditional approach, you'll be tempted to tell your players how to play the game and not waste time asking them questions. Resist this powerful temptation to tell them what to do, and especially don't do so before they begin to play the game.

If your players have trouble understanding what to do, phrase your questions to let them choose between one option versus another. For example, if you ask them "What's the fastest way to get the ball down the field?" and get answers such as "Throw it" or "Hit it," then ask, "Is it passing or dribbling?"

Immediately following the question-and-answer session you will begin a skill practice, which is Step 3 of the four-step process.

Sometimes players simply need to have more time playing the game, or you may need to modify the game further so that it is even easier for them to discover what they are to do. It'll take more patience on your part, but it's a powerful way to learn. Don't be reluctant to change the numbers in the teams or some aspect of the structure of the game to aid this discovery. In fact, we advocate playing "lopsided" games (e.g., 3 v 1, 3 v 2) in the second game of each practice; we'll explain this concept in a moment.

Step 3. Teach the Skills of the Game

Only when your players recognize the skills they need to be successful in the game do you want to teach the specific skills through focused drills. This is when you use a more traditional approach to teaching sport skills, the "IDEA" approach, which we will describe in chapter 5.

Step 4. Practice the Skills in Another Game

Once the players have practiced the skill, you then put them in another game situation—this time a lopsided game (e.g., 3 v 1, 3 v 2). Why use lopsided teams? It's simple: As a coach, you want your players to experience success as they're learning skills. The best way to experience success early on is to create an advantage for the players. This makes it more likely that, for instance, in a 3 v 1 game, your three offensive players will be able to make four passes before attempting to score.

We recommend using even-sided games (e.g., 3 v 3, 6 v 6) and then lopsided games. The reasoning behind this is to introduce players to a situation similar to what they will experience in competition, and to let them discover the challenges they face in performing the necessary skill. Then you teach them the skill, have them practice it, and put them back in another game—this time a lopsided one to give them a greater chance of experiencing success.

As players improve their skills you don't need to use lopsided games. At a certain point having a 3 v 1 or 6 v 3 advantage will be too easy for the kids and won't challenge them to hone their skills. At that point you lessen the advantage to, say, 3 v 2 or 6 v 4, or you may even decide that they're ready to practice the skill in even-sided competition. The key is to set up situations where your athletes experience success, yet are challenged in doing so. This will take careful monitoring on your part, but having kids play lopsided games as they are learning skills is a very effective way of helping them learn and improve.

And that's the games approach. Your players will get to *play* more in practice, and once they learn how the skills fit into their performance and enjoyment of the game, they'll be more motivated to work on those skills, which will help them to be successful.

chapter 5

Teaching and Shaping Skills

Coaching soccer is about teaching tactics, skills, fitness, values, and other useful things. It's also about "coaching" players before, during, and after contests. Teaching and coaching are closely related, but there are important differences. In this chapter we'll focus on principles of teaching, especially on teaching soccer skills. But many of the principles we'll discuss apply to teaching tactics, fitness concepts, and values as well. (Most of the other important teaching principles deal with communication, covered in chapter 2.) Then in chapter 6 we'll discuss the principles of coaching, which refer to your leadership activities during contests.

Teaching Soccer Skills

Many people believe that the only qualification needed to teach a skill is to have performed it. It's helpful to have performed it, but there is much more than that to teaching successfully. And even if you haven't performed the skill before, you can still learn to teach successfully with the useful acronym IDEA:

I – Introduce the skill.
D – Demonstrate the skill.
E – Explain the skill.
A – Attend to players practicing the skill.

These are the basic steps of good teaching. Now we'll explain each step in greater detail.

Introduce the Skill

Players, especially young and inexperienced ones, need to know what skill they are learning and why they are learning it. You should therefore take these three steps every time you introduce a skill to your players:

1. Get your players' attention.
2. Name the skill.
3. Explain the importance of the skill.

Get Your Players' Attention

Because youngsters are easily distracted, use some method to get their attention. Some coaches use interesting news items or stories. Others use jokes. And still others simply project enthusiasm to get their players to listen. Whatever method you use, speak slightly above the normal volume and look your players in the eye when you speak.

Also, position players so they can see and hear you. Arrange the players in two or three evenly spaced rows, facing you. (Make sure they aren't looking into the sun or at some distracting activity.) Then ask whether all of them can see you before you begin.

Name the Skill

Although you might mention other common names for the skill, decide which one you'll use and stick with it. This will help avoid confusion and enhance communication among your players.

Explain the Importance of the Skill

Although the importance of a skill may be apparent to you, your players may be less able to see how the skill will help them become better soccer players. Offer them a reason for learning the skill and describe how the skill relates to more advanced skills.

> *The most difficult aspect of coaching is this: Coaches must learn to let athletes learn. Sport skills should be taught so they have meaning to the child, not just meaning to the coach.*
>
> —Rainer Martens
> Founder of the American Sport Education Program

Demonstrate the Skill

The demonstration step is the most important part of teaching sport skills to players who may never have done anything closely resembling the skill. They need a picture, not just words. They need to see how the skill is performed.

If you are unable to perform the skill correctly, have an assistant coach, one of your players, or someone else more skilled perform the demonstration. These tips will help make your demonstrations more effective:

- Use correct form.
- Demonstrate the skill several times.
- Slow down the action, if possible, during one or two performances so players can see every movement involved in the skill.
- Perform the skill at different angles so your players can get a full perspective of it.
- Demonstrate the skill with both the right and the left legs.

Explain the Skill

Players learn more effectively when they're given a brief explanation of the skill along with the demonstration. Use simple terms and, if possible, relate the skill to previously learned skills. Ask your players whether they understand your description. A good technique is to ask the team to repeat your explanation. Ask questions like "What are you going to do first?" and "Then what?" Watch for when players look confused or uncertain, and repeat your explanation and demonstration at those points. If possible, use different words so your players get a chance to try to understand the skill from a different perspective.

Complex skills often are better understood when they are explained in more manageable parts. For instance, if you want to teach your players how to change direction when they dribble the ball, you might take the following steps:

1. Show them a correct performance of the entire skill, and explain its function in soccer.
2. Break down the skill and point out its component parts to your players.
3. Have players perform each of the component skills you have already taught them, such as dribbling while running, changing speed, and changing direction.
4. After players have demonstrated their ability to perform the separate parts of the skill in sequence, reexplain the entire skill.
5. Have players practice the skill in game-like conditions.

One caution: Young players have short attention spans, and a long demonstration or explanation of the skill will bore them. So spend no more than a few minutes altogether on the introduction, demonstration, and explanation phases. Then get the players active in a game that calls on them to perform the skill. The total IDEA should be completed in 10 minutes or less, followed by games in which players practice the skill.

Attend to Players Practicing the Skill

If the skill you selected was within your players' capabilities and you have done an effective job of introducing, demonstrating, and explaining it, your players should be ready to attempt the skill. Some players may need to be physically guided through the movements during their first few attempts. Walking unsure athletes through the skill in this way will help them gain confidence to perform the skill on their own.

Your teaching duties don't end when all your athletes have demonstrated that they understand how to perform the skill. In fact, a significant part of your teaching will involve observing closely the hit-and-miss trial performances of your players. In the next section we'll guide you in shaping players' skills, and then we'll help you learn how to detect and correct errors, using positive feedback. Keep in mind that your feedback will have a great influence on your players' motivation to practice and improve their performances.

Remember, too, that players need individual instruction. So set aside a time before, during, or after practice to give individual help.

Helping Players Improve Skills

After you have successfully taught your players the fundamentals of a skill, your focus will be on helping them improve that skill. Players will learn skills and improve upon them at different rates, so don't get too frustrated. Instead, help them improve by shaping their skills and detecting and correcting errors.

Shaping Players' Skills

One of your principal teaching duties is to reward positive behavior—in terms of successful skill execution—when you see it. A player makes a good pass in practice, and you immediately say, "That's the way to drive through it! Good follow through!" This, plus a smile and a "thumbs-up" gesture, go a long way toward reinforcing that technique in that player.

However, sometimes you may have a long, dry spell before you have any correct technique to reinforce. It's difficult to reward players when they aren't executing skills correctly. How can you shape their skills if this is the case?

Shaping skills takes practice on your players' part and patience on your part. Expect your players to make errors. Telling the player who made the great pass that she did a good job doesn't ensure that she'll make that pass the next time. Seeing inconsistency in your players' techniques can be frustrating. It's even more challenging to stay positive when your athletes repeatedly perform a skill incorrectly or lack enthusiasm for learning. It can certainly be frustrating to see athletes who seemingly don't heed your advice and continue to make the same mistakes. And when the athletes don't seem to care, you may wonder why you should.

Please know that it is normal to get frustrated at times when teaching skills. Nevertheless, part of successful coaching is controlling this frustration. Instead of getting upset, use these six guidelines for shaping skills:

1. **Think small initially.** Reward the first signs of behavior that approximate what you want. Then reward closer and closer approximations of the desired behavior. In short, use your reward power to shape the behavior you seek.

2. **Break skills into small steps.** For instance, in learning to dribble, one of your players does well in watching for defenders around the ball, but he's careless with the ball and doesn't effectively shield it from defenders. He often has the ball too far away from him as he dribbles, or runs too fast and loses control of it. Reinforce the correct technique of watching for defenders, and teach him how to keep the ball close. When he masters that, focus on getting him to run at a speed at which he can control the ball.

3. **Develop one component of a skill at a time.** Don't try to shape two components of a skill at once. For example, in receiving a ball with the thigh, players must stop the ball first and then control it by trapping it with the foot. Players should focus first on one aspect (stopping the ball with the thigh, cushioning it by dropping the knee slightly), then on the other (controlling it by trapping it with the foot). Athletes who have problems mastering a skill often do so because they're trying to improve two or more components at once. Help these athletes to isolate a single component.

4. **As athletes become more proficient at a skill, reinforce them only occasionally and only for the best examples of the skill behavior.** By focusing only on the best examples, you will help them continue to improve once they've mastered the basics.

5. **When athletes are trying to master a new skill, temporarily relax your standards for how you reward them.** As they focus on the new skill or attempt to integrate it with other skills, the old, well-learned skills may temporarily degenerate.

6. **If, however, a well-learned skill degenerates for long, you may need to restore it by going back to the basics.**

Coaches often have more skilled players provide feedback to teammates as they practice skills. This can be effective, but proceed with caution: You must tell the skilled players exactly what to look for when their teammates are performing the skills. You must also tell them the corrections for the common errors of that skill.

We've looked at how to guide your athletes as they learn skills. Now let's look at another critical teaching principle that you should employ as you're shaping skills: detecting and correcting errors.

Detecting and Correcting Errors

Good coaches recognize that athletes make two types of errors: learning errors and performance errors. *Learning errors* are ones that occur because athletes don't know how to perform a skill; that is, they have not yet developed the correct motor program in the brain to perform a particular skill. *Performance errors* are made not because athletes don't know how to do the skill, but because they have made a mistake in executing what they do know. There is no easy way to know whether a player is making learning or performance errors. Part of the art of coaching is being able to sort out which type of error each mistake is.

The process of helping your athletes correct errors begins with your observing and evaluating their performances to determine whether the mistakes are learning or performance errors. For performance errors, you need to look for the reasons that your athletes are not performing as well as they know how. If the mistakes are learning errors, then you need to help them learn the skill, which is the focus of this section.

There is no substitute for knowing skills well in correcting learning errors. The better you understand a skill—not only how it is done correctly but also what causes learning errors—the more helpful you will be in correcting mistakes.

One of the most common coaching mistakes is to provide inaccurate feedback and advice on how to correct errors. Don't rush into error correction; wrong feedback or poor advice will hurt the learning process more than no feedback or advice. If you are uncertain about the cause of the problem or how to correct it, continue to observe and analyze until you are more sure. As a rule, you should see the error repeated several times before attempting to correct it.

Correct One Error at a Time

Suppose Jill, one of your forwards, is having trouble with her shooting. She's doing most things well, but you notice that she's not keeping her foot pointed down as she strikes the ball, and she often approaches the ball sort of sideways, her hips not square to the target. What do you do?

First, decide which error to correct first, because athletes learn more effectively when they attempt to correct one error at a time. Determine whether one error is causing the other; if so, have the athlete correct that error first, because it may eliminate the other error. In Jill's case, however, neither error is causing the other. In such cases, athletes should correct the error that will bring the greatest improvement when remedied—for Jill, this probably means kicking with the foot pointed down. Improvement here will likely motivate her to correct the other error.

Use Positive Feedback to Correct Errors

The positive approach to correcting errors includes emphasizing what to do instead of what not to do. Use compliments, praise, rewards, and encouragement to correct errors. Acknowledge correct performance as well as efforts to improve. By using the positive approach, you can help your athletes feel good about themselves and promote a strong desire to achieve.

When you're working with one athlete at a time, the positive approach to correcting errors includes four steps:

1. Praise effort and correct performance.
2. Give simple and precise feedback to correct errors.
3. Make sure the athlete understands your feedback.
4. Provide an environment that motivates the athlete to improve.

Let's take a brief look at each step.

Step 1: Praise Effort and Correct Performance. Praise your athlete for trying to perform a skill correctly and for performing any parts of it correctly. Praise the athlete immediately after he or she performs the skill, if possible. Keep the praise simple: "Good try," "Way to hustle," or "Good form," "Good extension," "That's the way to follow through." You can also use nonverbal feedback, such as smiling, clapping your hands, or any facial or body expression that shows approval.

Make sure you're sincere with your praise. Don't indicate that an athlete's effort was good when it wasn't. Usually an athlete knows when he or she has made a sincere effort to perform the skill correctly and perceives undeserved praise for what it is—untruthful feedback to make him or her feel good. Likewise, don't indicate that a player's performance was correct when it wasn't.

Step 2: Give Simple and Precise Feedback. Don't burden a player with a long or detailed explanation of how to correct an error. Give just enough feedback so the player can correct one error at a time. Before giving feedback, recognize that some athletes will readily accept it immediately after the error; others will respond better if you slightly delay the correction.

For errors that are complicated to explain and difficult to correct, try the following:

- Explain and demonstrate what the athlete should have done. Do not demonstrate what the athlete did wrong.
- Explain the cause or causes of the error, if this isn't obvious.
- Explain why you are recommending the correction you have selected, if it's not obvious.

Step 3: Make Sure the Athlete Understands Your Feedback. If the athlete doesn't understand your feedback, he or she won't be able to correct the error. Ask him or her to repeat the feedback and to explain and demonstrate how it will be used. If the athlete can't do this, be patient and present your feedback again. Then have the athlete repeat the feedback after you're finished.

Step 4: Provide an Environment That Motivates the Athlete to Improve. Your players won't always be able to correct their errors immediately even if they do understand your feedback. Encourage them to "hang tough" and stick with it when corrections are difficult or they seem discouraged. For more difficult corrections, remind them that it will take time, and the improvement will happen only if they work at it. Look to encourage players with low self-confidence. Saying something like, "You were dribbling at a much better speed today; with practice, you'll be able to keep the ball closer to you and shield it from defenders," can motivate a player to continue to refine his or her dribbling skills.

Some athletes need to be more motivated to improve. Others may be very self-motivated and need little help from you in this area at all; with them you can practically ignore step 4 when correcting an error. While motivation comes from within, look to provide an environment of positive instruction and encouragement to help your athletes improve.

A final note on correcting errors: Team sports such as soccer provide unique challenges in this endeavor. How do you provide individual feedback in a group setting using a positive approach? Instead of yelling across the field to correct an error (and embarrassing the player), substitute for the player who erred. Then make the correction on the sidelines. This type of feedback has three advantages:

- The player will be more receptive to the one-on-one feedback.
- The other players are still active, still practicing skills, and unable to hear your discussion.
- Because the rest of the team is still playing, you'll feel compelled to make your comments simple and concise—which, as we've said, is more helpful to the player.

This doesn't mean you can't use the team setting to give specific, positive feedback. You can do so to emphasize correct group and individual performances. Use this team feedback approach *only* for positive statements, though. Keep any negative feedback for individual discussions.

Developing Practice Plans

You will need to create practice plans for each season. Each practice plan should contain the following sections:

- Purpose
- Equipment
- Plan

Purpose sections focus on what you want to teach your players during each practice; they outline your main theme for each practice. The purpose should be drawn from your season plan (see chapter 9). Equipment sections note what you'll need to have on hand for that practice. Plan sections outline what you will do during each practice session. Each consists of these elements:

- Warm-up
- Games
- Skill practices
- Cool-down and wrap-up

You'll begin each session with about five minutes of warm-up activities. Then you'll have your players play a modified soccer game (look in chapter 8 for suggested games). You'll look for your cue to interrupt that game—your cue being when players are having problems with carrying out the basic goal or aim of the game. At this point you'll "freeze" the action, keeping the players where they are, and ask brief questions about the tactical problems the players encountered and what skills they need to solve those problems. (Review chapter 4 for more on interrupting a game and holding a question-and-answer session.)

Then you'll teach the skill the players need to acquire to successfully execute the tactic. During skill practice you'll use the IDEA approach:

- Introduce the skill.
- Demonstrate the skill.
- Explain the skill.
- Attend to players' practicing the skill.

Your introduction, demonstration, and explanation of a skill should take no more than two to three minutes; then you'll attend to players and provide teaching cues or further demonstration as necessary as they practice the skill.

After the Skill Practices, you will usually have the athletes play another game or two to let them use the skills they have just learned and to understand them in the context of a game. During Game and Skill Practices, emphasize the importance of every player on the field moving and being involved in every play, whether they will be directly touching the ball or backing up their teammates. No player on the field should be standing around.

The plan section continues with a cool-down and stretch. Following this you'll wrap up the practice with a few summary comments and remind them of the next practice or game day.

The games in chapter 8 include lists of suggestions to help you modify each game to make it easier or harder to play. These suggestions will help you keep practices fun and provide activities for players with varying skill levels.

Although practicing using the games approach should reduce the need for discipline, there will be times when you'll have to deal with players who are misbehaving in practice. In the next section we'll help you handle these situations.

Dealing With Misbehavior

Athletes will misbehave at times; it's only natural. Following are two ways you can respond to misbehavior: through extinction or discipline.

Extinction

Ignoring a misbehavior—neither rewarding nor disciplining it—is called *extinction*. This can be effective under certain circumstances. In some situations, disciplining young people's misbehavior only encourages them to act up further because of the recognition they get. Ignoring misbehavior teaches youngsters that it is not worth your attention.

Sometimes, though, you cannot wait for a behavior to fizzle out. When players cause danger to themselves or others or disrupt the activities of others, you need to take immediate action. Tell the offending player that the behavior must stop and that discipline will follow if it doesn't. If the athlete doesn't stop misbehaving after the warning, discipline.

Extinction also doesn't work well when a misbehavior is self-rewarding. For example, you may be able to keep from grimacing if a youngster kicks you in the shin, but he or she still knows you were hurt. Therein lies the reward. In these circumstances, it is also necessary to discipline the player for the undesirable behavior.

Extinction works best in situations in which players are seeking recognition through mischievous behaviors, clowning, or grandstanding. Usually, if you are patient, their failure to get your attention will cause the behavior to disappear.

However, be alert that you don't extinguish desirable behavior. When youngsters do something well, they expect to be positively reinforced. Not rewarding them will likely cause them to discontinue the desired behavior.

Discipline

Some educators say we should never discipline young people, but should only reinforce their positive behaviors. They argue that discipline does not work, it creates hostility, and sometimes develops avoidance behaviors that may be more unwholesome than the original problem behavior. It is true that discipline does not always work and that it can create problems when used ineffectively, but when used appropriately, discipline is effective in eliminating undesirable behaviors without creating other undesirable consequences. You must use discipline effectively, because it is impossible to guide athletes through positive reinforcement and extinction alone. Discipline is part of the positive approach when these guidelines are followed:

- Discipline in a corrective way to help athletes improve now and in the future. Don't discipline to retaliate and make yourself feel better.
- Impose discipline in an impersonal way when athletes break team rules or otherwise misbehave. Shouting at or scolding athletes indicates that your attitude is one of revenge.
- Once a good rule has been agreed on, ensure that athletes who violate it experience the unpleasant consequences of their misbehavior. Don't wave discipline threateningly over their heads. Just do it, but warn an athlete once before disciplining.
- Be consistent in administering discipline.
- Don't discipline using consequences that may cause you guilt. If you can't think of an appropriate consequence right away, tell the player you will talk with him or her after you think about it. You might consider involving the player in designing a consequence.
- Once the discipline is completed, don't make athletes feel they are "in the doghouse." Make them feel that they're valued members of the team again.

- Make sure that what you think is discipline isn't perceived by the athlete as a positive reinforcement—for instance, keeping a player out of doing a certain drill or portion of the practice may be just what the athlete desired.
- Never discipline athletes for making errors when they are playing.
- Never use physical activity—running laps or doing push-ups—as discipline. To do so only causes athletes to resent physical activity, something we want them to learn to enjoy throughout their lives.
- Discipline sparingly. Constant discipline and criticism cause athletes to turn their interests elsewhere and to resent you as well.

chapter 6

Game-Day Coaching

Contests provide the opportunity for your players to show what they've learned in practice. Just as your players' focus shifts on contest days from learning and practicing to *competing,* so your focus shifts from teaching skills to coaching players as they perform those skills in contests. Of course, the contest is a teaching opportunity as well, but the focus is on performing what has been previously learned.

In the last chapter you learned how to teach your players soccer tactics and skills; in this chapter we'll help you coach your players as they execute those tactics and skills in contests. We'll provide important coaching principles that will guide you throughout the game day—before, during, and after the contest.

Before the Contest

Just as you need a practice plan for what you're going to do each practice, you need a game plan for what to do on the day of a game. Many inexperienced coaches focus only on how they will coach during the contest itself, but your preparations to coach should include details that begin well before the first play of the game. In fact, your preparations should begin during the practice before the contest.

Preparations at Practice

During the practice a day or two before the next contest, you should do two things (besides practicing tactics and skills) to prepare your players: Decide on any specific team tactics that you want to employ, and discuss pregame particulars such as what to eat before the game, what to wear, and when to be at the field.

Deciding Team Tactics

Some coaches see themselves as great military strategists guiding their young warriors to victory on the battlefield. These coaches burn the midnight oil as they devise a complex plan of attack. There are several things wrong with this approach, but we'll point out two errors in terms of deciding team tactics:

1. The decision on team tactics should be made with input from players.
2. Team tactics at this level don't need to be complex.

Perhaps you guessed right on the second point but were surprised by the first. Why should you include your players in deciding tactics? Isn't that the coach's role?

It's the coach's role to help youngsters grow through the sport experience. Giving your athletes a chance to offer input here helps them to learn the game. It gets them involved at a planning level that often is reserved solely for the coach. It gives them a feeling of ownership; they're not just "carrying out orders" of the coach. They're executing the plan of attack that was jointly decided. Youngsters who have a say in how they approach a task often respond with more enthusiasm and motivation.

Don't dampen that enthusiasm and motivation by concocting tactics that are too complex. Keep tactics simple, especially at the younger levels. Focus on providing support, moving continuously, spreading out the attack, and passing and shooting often.

As you become more familiar with your team's tendencies and abilities, help players focus on specific tactics that will help them play better. For example, if team members have a tendency to stand around and watch the action, emphasize moving more and spreading out the attack. If they are active and moving throughout the game, but not in any cohesive fashion, focus them on providing support by using the triangle concept (see chapter 8).

If you're coaching 12- to 14-year-olds, you might institute certain plays that your team has practiced. These plays should take advantage of your players' strengths. Again, give the players the chance to provide input into what plays might be employed in a game.

Discussing Precontest Particulars

Players need to know what to do before a contest: what they should eat on game day and when, what clothing they should wear to the game, what equipment they should bring, and what time they should arrive at the field. Discuss these particulars with them at the practice before a contest. Here are guidelines for discussing these issues.

Pregame Meal. Carbohydrates are easily digested and absorbed and are a ready source of fuel. Players should eat a high-carbohydrate meal ideally about three to four hours before a game to allow the stomach to empty completely. This won't be possible for games held in early morning; in this case, athletes should still eat food high in carbohydrates, such as an English muffin, toast, or cereal, but not so much that their stomachs are full. In addition, athletes' pregame meals shouldn't include foods that are spicy or high in fat content.

Clothing and Equipment. Instruct players to wear their team shirts or uniforms, shorts, knee-high stockings, suitable shoes, and soccer shin guards. All cleats, studs, or bars on shoes must be not less than ½-inch wide and not longer than ¾-inch. Aluminum, leather, rubber, nylon, and plastic cleats are legal.

Players may not wear equipment with projecting metal or other hard plates or with exposed sharp edges. They also may not wear pads containing hard or unyielding materials, even if covered with soft padding.

Time to Arrive. Your players will need to adequately warm up before a game, so instruct them to arrive 20 minutes before a game to go through a team warm-up (see "The Warm-Up" later in this chapter).

Facilities, Equipment, and Support Personnel

Although the site coordinator and officials have responsibilities regarding facilities and equipment, it's wise for you to know what to look for to make sure the contest is safe for the athletes. You should arrive at the field 25 to 30 minutes before game time so you can check the field, check in with the site coordinator and officials, and greet your players as they arrive to warm up. The site coordinator and officials should be checking the facilities and preparing for the contest. If officials aren't arriving before the game when they're supposed to, inform the site coordinator. A facilities checklist includes the following:

Field surface

- ✔ Sprinkler heads and openings are at grass level.
- ✔ The field is free of toxic substances (lime, fertilizer, and so on).
- ✔ The field is free of low spots or ruts.
- ✔ The playing surface is free of debris.
- ✔ No rocks or cement slabs are on the field.
- ✔ The field is free of protruding pipes, wires, and lines.
- ✔ The field is not too wet.
- ✔ The field is not too dry.
- ✔ The field lines are well marked.

Outside playing area

- ✔ The edge of the playing field is at least six feet from trees, walls, fences, and cars.
- ✔ Nearby buildings are protected (by fences, walls) from possible damage during play.
- ✔ Storage sheds and facilities are locked.
- ✔ The playground area (ground surface and equipment) is in safe condition.
- ✔ The fences/walls lining the area are in good repair.
- ✔ Sidewalks are without cracks, separations, or raised concrete.

Equipment

- ✔ Goals are held securely together.
- ✔ Goals are secured to the ground.

Regarding equipment, also make sure players have brought their shin guards with them. Consider carrying an extra pair or two, to be returned to you after games, in case a player forgets his or her own.

Communicating With Parents

The groundwork for your communication with parents will have been laid in the parent orientation meeting, through which parents learn the best ways to support their kids'—and the whole team's—efforts on the field. As parents gather at the field before a contest, let them know what the team has been focusing on during the past week and what your goals are for the game. For instance, perhaps you've worked on the "give-and-go" play in practice this week; encourage parents to watch for improvement and success in executing this play and to support the team members as they attempt all tactics and skills. Help parents to judge success not just based on the contest outcome, but on how the kids are improving their performances.

If parents yell at the kids for mistakes made during the game, make disparaging remarks about the officials or opponents, or shout instructions on what tactics to employ, ask them to refrain from making such remarks and to instead be supportive of the team in their comments and actions.

After a contest, briefly and informally assess with parents, as the opportunity arises, how the team did based not on the outcome, but on meeting performance goals and playing to the best of their abilities. Help parents see the contest as a process, not solely as a test that's pass/fail or win/lose. Encourage parents to reinforce that concept at home.

Unplanned Events

Part of being prepared to coach is to expect the unexpected. What do you do if players are late? What if *you* have an emergency and can't make the game or will be late? What if the contest is rained out or otherwise postponed? Being prepared to handle out-of-the-ordinary circumstances will help you when such unplanned events happen.

If players are late, you may have to adjust your starting lineup. While this may not be a major inconvenience, do stress to your players the importance of being on time for two reasons:

- Part of being a member of a team means being committed and responsible to the other members. When players don't show up, or show up late, they break that commitment.
- Players need to go through a warm-up to physically prepare for the contest. Skipping the warm-up risks injury.

Consider making a team rule stating that players need to show up 20 minutes before a game and go through the complete team warm-up, or they won't start.

An emergency might cause *you* to be late or miss a game. In such cases, notify your assistant coach, if you have one, or the league coordinator. If notified in advance, a parent of a player or another volunteer might be able to step in for the contest.

Sometimes a game will be postponed because of inclement weather or for other reasons (such as unsafe field conditions). If the postponement takes place before game day, you'll need to call each member of your team to let him or her know. If it happens while the teams are on the field preparing for the game, gather your team members and tell them the news and why the game is being postponed. Make sure all your players have rides home before you leave—be the last to leave to be sure.

The Warm-Up

Players need to both physically and mentally prepare for a game once they arrive at the field. Physical preparation involves warming up. We've suggested that players arrive 20 minutes before the game to warm up. Conduct the warm-up similar to practice warm-ups, with some brief games that focus on skill practice and stretching.

Players should prepare to do what they will do in the game: dribble, pass, receive, shoot, mark, tackle, and goalkeep. This doesn't mean they spend extensive time on each skill; you can plan two or three brief practice games that encompass all these skills.

After playing a few brief games, your players should stretch. You don't need to deliver any big pep talk, but you can help your players mentally prepare as they stretch by reminding them of the following:

- The tactics and skills they've been working on in recent practices, especially focusing their attention on what they've been doing well. Focus on their strengths.
- The team tactics you decided on in your previous practice.
- Performing the tactics and skills to the best of their individual abilities and playing together as a team.
- Playing hard and smart and having fun!

During the Contest

The list you just read goes a long way toward defining your focus for coaching during the contest. Throughout the game, you'll keep the game in proper perspective and help your players do the same. You'll observe how your players execute tactics and skills and how well they play together. You'll make tactical decisions in a number of areas. You'll model appropriate behavior on the sideline, showing respect for opponents and officials, and demand the same of your athletes. You'll watch out for your athletes' physical safety and psychological welfare, in terms of building their self-esteem and helping them manage stress and anxiety.

Proper Perspective

Winning games is the short-term goal of your soccer program; helping your players learn the tactics, skills, and rules of soccer, how to become fit, and how to be good sports in soccer and in life is the long-term goal. Your young athletes are "winning" when they are becoming better human beings through their participation in soccer. Keep that perspective in mind when you coach. *You* have the privilege of setting the tone for how your team approaches the game. Keep winning and all aspects of the competition in proper perspective, and your young charges will likely follow suit.

Tactical Decisions

While you aren't called upon to be a great military strategist, you are called upon to make tactical decisions in several areas throughout a contest. You'll make decisions about who starts the game and when to enter substitutes, about making slight adjustments to your team's tactics, and about correcting players' performance errors or leaving the correction for the next practice.

Starting and Substituting Players

In considering playing time, make sure that everyone on the team gets to play at least half of each game. This should be your guiding principle as you consider starting and substitution patterns. We suggest you consider two options in substituting players:

- **Substituting individually.** Replace one player with another. This offers you a lot of latitude in deciding who goes in when, and it gives you the greatest mix of players throughout the game, but it can be hard to keep track of playing time (this could be made easier by assigning an assistant or a parent to this task). Remember that each player is required to play one half of each game.

⊙ **Substituting by quarters.** The advantage here is that you can easily track playing time, and players know how long they will be in before they might be replaced.

Adjusting Team Tactics

At the 8 to 9 and 10 to 11 age levels, you probably won't adjust your team tactics too significantly during a game; rather, you'll focus on the basic tactics in general and emphasize during breaks which tactics your team needs to work on in particular. However, coaches of 12- to 14-year-olds might have cause to make tactical adjustments to improve their team's chances of performing well and winning. As games progress, assess your opponents' style of play and tactics, and make adjustments that are appropriate—that is, that your players are prepared for. Consider the following examples:

How do your opponents usually initiate their attack? Do they aim to get around, over, or through your defense? This can help you make defensive adjustments.

Who are the strongest players on the opposing team? The weakest players? As you identify strong players, you'll want to assign more skilled players to mark them.

Are the forwards fast and powerful? Do they come to the ball, or do they try to run behind the defense and receive passes? Their mode of attack should influence how you instruct your players to mark them.

On defense, do your opponents play a high-pressure game, or do they retreat once you've gained possession of the ball? Either type of defense could call for a different strategy from you. Knowing the answers to such questions can help you both formulate a game plan and make adjustments during a game.

However, don't stress tactics too much during a game. Doing so can take the fun out of the game for the players. If you don't trust your memory, carry a pen and notepad to note which team tactics and individual skills need attention in the next practice.

Correcting Players' Errors

In chapter 5 you learned about two types of errors: learning errors and performance errors. Learning errors are ones that occur because athletes don't know how to perform a skill. Athletes make performance errors not because they don't know how to do the skill, but because they make a mistake in executing what they do know.

Sometimes it's not easy to tell which type of error athletes are making. Knowing your athletes' capabilities helps you to know whether they know the skill and are simply making mistakes in executing it or whether they don't really know how to perform the skill. If they are making learning errors—that is, they don't know how to perform the skills—you'll need to make note of this and teach them at the next practice. Game time is not the time to teach skills.

If they are making performance errors, however, you can help players correct those errors during a game. Players who make performance errors often do so because they have a lapse in concentration or motivation—or they are simply demonstrating the human quality of sometimes doing things incorrectly. A word of encouragement to concentrate more may help. If you do correct a performance error during a contest, do so in a quiet, controlled, and positive tone of voice during a break or when the player is on the sidelines with you.

For those making performance errors, you have to decide if it is just the occasional error anyone makes or an expected error for a youngster at that stage of development. If that is the case, then the player may appreciate your not commenting on the mistake. The player knows it was a mistake and knows how to correct it. On the other hand, perhaps an encouraging word and a "coaching cue" (such as "Remember to follow through on your shots") may be just what the athlete needs. Knowing the players and what to say is very much a part of the "art" of coaching.

Coach's and Players' Behavior

Another aspect of coaching on game day is managing behavior—both yours and your athletes'. The two are closely connected.

Your Conduct

You very much influence your players' behavior before, during, and after a contest. If you're up, your players are more likely to be up. If you're anxious, they'll notice and the anxiety can be contagious. If you're negative, they'll respond with worry. If you're positive, they'll play with more enjoyment. If you're constantly yelling instructions or commenting on mistakes and errors, it will be difficult for players to concentrate. Instead, let players get into the flow of the game.

The focus should be on positive competition and on having fun. A coach who overorganizes everything and dominates a game from the sideline is definitely *not* making the contest fun.

So how should you conduct yourself on the sideline? Here are a few pointers:

- Be calm, in control, and supportive of your players.

- Encourage players often, but instruct during play sparingly. Players should be focusing on their performance during a game, not on instructions shouted from the sidelines.
- If you need to instruct a player, do so when you're both on the sidelines, in an unobtrusive manner. Never yell at players for making a mistake. Instead, briefly demonstrate or remind them of the correct technique and encourage them.

Remember, you're not playing for the World Cup! In this program, soccer competitions are designed to help players develop their skills and themselves—and to have fun. So coach in a manner at games that helps your players do those things.

Players' Conduct

You're responsible for keeping your players under control. Do so by setting a good example and by disciplining when necessary. Set team rules of good behavior. If players attempt to cheat, fight, argue, badger, yell disparaging remarks, and the like, it is your responsibility to correct the misbehavior. Consider team rules in these areas of game conduct:

- Players' language
- Players' behavior
- Interactions with officials
- Discipline for misbehavior
- Dress code for competitions

Players' Physical Safety

We devoted all of chapter 3 to discussing how to provide for players' safety, but it's worth noting here that safety during contests can be affected by how officials are calling the rules. If they aren't calling rules correctly, and this risks injury to your players, you must intervene. Voice your concern in a respectful manner and in a way that places the emphasis where it should be: on the athletes' safety. One of the officials' main responsibilities is to provide for athletes' safety; you are not adversaries here. Don't hesitate to address an issue of safety with an official when the need arises.

Players' Psychological Welfare

Athletes often attach their self-worth to winning and losing. This idea is fueled by coaches, parents, peers, and society, who place great emphasis on winning. Players become anxious when they're uncertain if they can meet the expectations of others or of themselves when meeting these expectations is important to them.

If you place too much importance on the game or cause your athletes to doubt their abilities, they will become anxious about the outcome and their performance. If your players look uptight and anxious during a contest, find ways to reduce both the uncertainties about how their performance will be evaluated and the importance they are attaching to the game. Help athletes focus on realistic personal goals—goals that are reachable and measurable and that will help them improve their performance. Another way to reduce anxiety on game day is to stay away from emotional pregame pep talks. We provided guidance earlier in what to address before the game.

When coaching during contests, remember that the most important outcome from playing soccer is to build or enhance players' self-worth. Keep that firmly in mind, and strive to make every coaching decision promote your athletes' self-worth.

Opponents and Officials

Respect opponents and officials. Without them, you wouldn't have a competition. Officials help provide a fair and safe experience for athletes and, as appropriate, help them learn the game. Opponents provide opportunities for your team to test itself, improve, and excel.

You and your team should show respect for opponents by giving your best efforts. You owe them this. Showing respect doesn't necessarily mean being "nice" to your opponents, though it does mean being civil.

Don't allow your players to "trash talk" or taunt an opponent. Such behavior is disrespectful to the spirit of the competition and to the opponent. Immediately remove a player from a contest if he or she disobeys your orders in this area.

Remember that officials are quite often teenagers—in many cases not much older than the players themselves. The level of officiating should be commensurate to the level of play. In other words, don't expect perfection from officials any more than you do from your own players. Especially at younger levels, they *won't* make every call, because to do so would stop the contest every 10 seconds.

After the Contest

When the game is over, join your team in congratulating the coaches and players of the opposing team, then be sure to thank the officials.

Check on any injuries players sustained and let players know how to care for them. Be prepared to speak with the officials about any problems that occurred during the game. Then hold a brief Team Circle, as explained in a moment, to ensure your players are on an even keel, whether they won or lost.

Winning With Class, Losing With Dignity

When celebrating a victory, make sure your team does so in a way that doesn't show disrespect for the opponents. It's fine and appropriate to be happy and celebrate a win, but don't allow your players to taunt the opponents or boast about their victory. Keep winning in perspective. Winning and losing are a part of life, not just a part of sport. If players can handle both equally well, they'll be successful in whatever they do.

Athletes are competitors, and competitors will be disappointed in defeat. If your team has made a winning effort, let them know that. After a loss, help them keep their chins up and maintain a positive attitude that will carry over into the next practice and contest.

Team Circle

If your players have performed well in a game, compliment them and congratulate them immediately afterward. Tell them specifically what they did well, whether they won or lost. This will reinforce their desire to repeat their good performances.

Don't criticize individual players for poor performances in front of teammates. Help players improve their skills, but do so in the next practice, not immediately after a game.

The postgame Team Circle isn't the time to go over tactical problems and adjustments. The players are either so happy after a win or so dejected after a loss that they won't absorb much tactical information immediately following a game. Your first concern should be your players' attitudes and mental well-being. You don't want them to be too high after a win or too low after a loss. This is the time you can be most influential in keeping the outcome in perspective and keeping them on an even keel.

Finally, make sure your players have transportation home. Be the last one to leave in order to help if transportation falls through and to ensure full supervision of players before they leave.

chapter 7

Rules and Equipment

This is where we'll introduce you to some of the basic rules of soccer. We won't try to cover all the rules of the game but rather will give you what you need to work with players who are 8 to 14 years old. We'll give you information on equipment and field size and markings, actions to start and restart the game, fouls, and scoring rules. We recommend you use these rules, many of which have been modified from the adult version of the game to make the sport more appropriate for youngsters. In a short section at the end of the chapter we'll show you the officiating signals for soccer.

Basic Rules

In table 7.1 we present rules that cover many of the basics of the game. Figure 7.1 shows the field markings for a soccer field.

Players need little in the way of playing equipment for themselves. Multi-studded soccer shoes are recommended for outdoor play, but they are not required. Clothing should be loose-fitting and appropriate for

Table 7.1 Rule Modifications for Soccer

Item	8- to 9-year-olds	10- to 11-year-olds	12- to 14-year-olds
Players on team	10	12	16
Ball size	3	4	4
Goal size	6 feet high × 16 feet wide	6 feet × 16 feet	8 feet × 24 feet
Field size	60 yards long × 40 yards wide	70 yards × 50 yards	110 yards × 70 yards
Players on field	6 v 6	8 v 8	11 v 11
Length of game	40 minutes (in quarters)	50 minutes (in halves)	70 minutes (in halves)

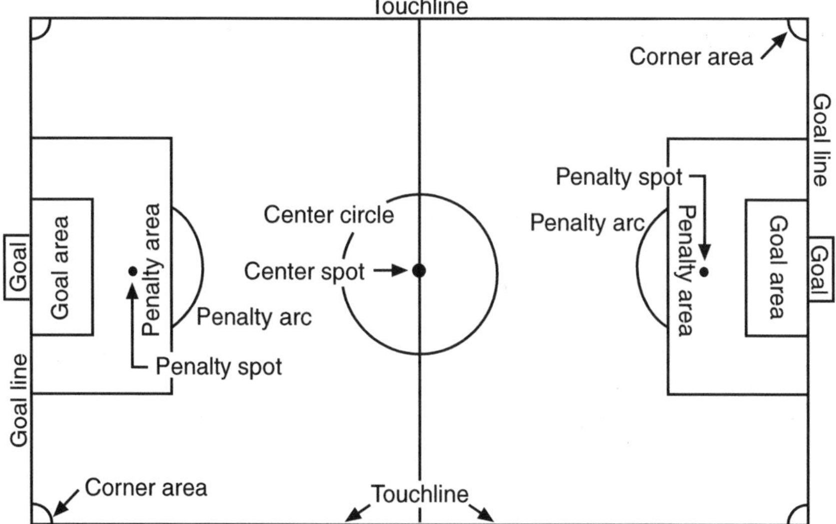

Figure 7.1 Soccer field markings.

the weather. Shin guards, provided by the players, should be worn under knee-length socks to protect players' legs. Goalkeepers should wear protective gloves.

Player Positions

All players should get to practice and play at all positions—not necessarily in every game, but throughout the season. Here is a brief description of each position.

- **Forwards.** Forwards play closer to the other team's goal and shoot the ball more than do other players. The forwards that play nearest the touchlines are called "wings"; those in the middle of the field are referred to as "strikers."
- **Midfielders.** Midfielders are all-purpose players who take shots and also try to steal the ball from the other team. They are transition players, helping move the ball from defense to offense. Their position is named appropriately, as they are located between forwards and defenders on the field.
- **Defenders.** Defenders play near their own team's goal and try to prevent the other team from shooting the ball. They also receive the ball from the goalie and move the ball up the field to begin the offense.
- **Goalkeeper.** A goalie plays in front of the goal and tries to prevent the ball from getting into the goal. The goalie is the only player allowed to use hands to block shots and initiate the offense from within the penalty area.

Typical alignments for games at various levels are noted in table 7.2; the goalkeeper is always assumed.

Note that these are not the only formations that can work with your players. To increase scoring chances, you can move one of your midfielders to a forward position. Use the formation that best suits your team's strengths and weaknesses.

Table 7.2 Typical Alignments

	6 v 6	8 v 8	11 v 11
Defenders	2	3	4
Midfielders	2	3	4
Forwards	1	1	2

Starting and Restarting the Game

Specific procedures are used to start a game of soccer and to restart it following the ball going out of bounds. The start is done as a center kickoff; restarts of the game, which occur after the ball goes out of bounds, can be a goal kick, a corner kick, or a throw-in, depending on the situation.

Center Kickoff

Soccer games begin with one team kicking the ball from the center spot. (The team is often chosen by a coin toss.) The opposing team's players are not allowed within the center circle during the kickoff. Players on both teams must be on their half of the field during the kickoff, and the kicked ball must roll forward at least one complete rotation before another player may touch it.

These same procedures are followed after a goal is scored. In this situation, the team that was scored upon restarts the game by kicking off from the center spot, and the team that scored stands outside of the center circle in its half of the field.

Goal Kick

When an attacking team kicks the ball out of bounds beyond the goal line, as in a missed shot, the opposing team is awarded a free kick called a *goal kick.* This kick is made by the defending team and must be made inside the goal box on the side of the goal on which the ball went out of play. The players on the team that kicked the ball out of bounds must stay outside the penalty area until the ball clears the area (see figure 7.2).

Corner Kick

If a team kicks the ball beyond its own goal line, the other team is awarded a corner kick from a corner arc. During the kick, defensive players must be at least 10 yards from the player kicking the ball. The kicker's teammates may position themselves anywhere they choose (see figure 7.3).

Throw-In

When the ball is kicked out of bounds along the touchline, the game is restarted with a throw-in (see figure 7.4). The team that last touched the ball loses possession, and the other team gets to throw in the ball.

Figure 7.2 Goal kick.

Figure 7.3 Corner kick.

The player putting the ball back into play must use both hands to throw the ball and keep both feet on the ground. The throwing motion should begin from behind the head and be a continuous forward thrust until the ball is released in front of the head. The throw-in should be put into play quickly, thrown to the feet of a player who is not being marked (guarded).

Figure 7.4 Proper technique for a throw-in.

Fouls

Fouls are called when one player runs into, charges, pushes, trips, kicks, or holds an opposing player. A handball foul is called when a player intentionally touches the ball with his or her hand or arm to gain control.

Players who continually intentionally foul or play dangerously are warned once by the official, who presents them with a yellow card. The next time they intentionally foul or play dangerously, they receive a red card and are ejected from the game. Officials also can eject a player without warning if they rule a behavior unacceptable.

Two kinds of kicks can be awarded for fouls, based on where the foul is committed: direct free kicks or indirect free kicks.

Direct and Indirect Free Kicks

Fouls usually result in either a direct or an indirect free kick. The type of foul committed determines which of the two is awarded (see table 7.3). Direct free kicks may be kicked directly at the goal, whereas indirect free kicks must touch another player before a goal can be scored. Opponents must be at least 10 yards away from the ball during a free kick. Any free kick awarded within a defending team's own goal area may be taken from any point within the goal area. An indirect free kick awarded to the attacking team within the opponent's goal area will be taken from the goal-area line nearest to the point of infraction. The officials will signal which type of free kick has been awarded.

Table 7.3 Free Kick Fouls

Direct kick	Indirect kick
Handball	Playing dangerously
Kicking an opponent	Obstructing an opponent
Striking an opponent	Goalkeeper taking too many steps (four or more)
Tripping an opponent	Offside
Holding an opponent	
Pushing an opponent	
Jumping at an opponent	
Charging into an opponent	
Charging from behind	

Penalty Kicks

Penalty kicks are awarded to the attacking team if a defending player commits a direct-kick foul inside the penalty area. A penalty kick is a free shot at the goal by an individual attacker with only the goalkeeper defending against the shot. Penalty kicks are taken 12 yards in front of the center of the goal (see figure 7.5). The goalkeeper may not leave the line until after the ball is kicked.

Figure 7.5 Proper setup for a penalty kick.

Offside

An offside foul is called when a teammate tries to pass the ball to a player in the offside position. A player is in the offside position when he or she is closer to the opponent's goal than at least two defensive players, including the goalie, when the ball is passed forward (see figure 7.6). The offside rule prevents offensive players from simply waiting at the goal mouth for an easy shot, but it does not apply to throw-ins, corner kicks, or when players are in their own half of the field.

Note that a player is not called offside for merely being in an offside position. The player must be participating in the play to be ruled offside (see figure 7.7). For example, if play is occurring on one side of the field, and a player on the other side of the field is in an offside position but is not involved in the play going on across the field (e.g., a teammate is not passing or attempting to pass to her), then that player won't

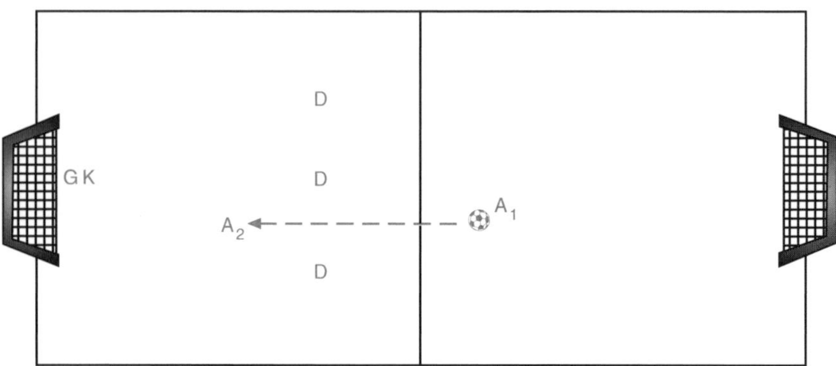

Figure 7.6 Offside foul.

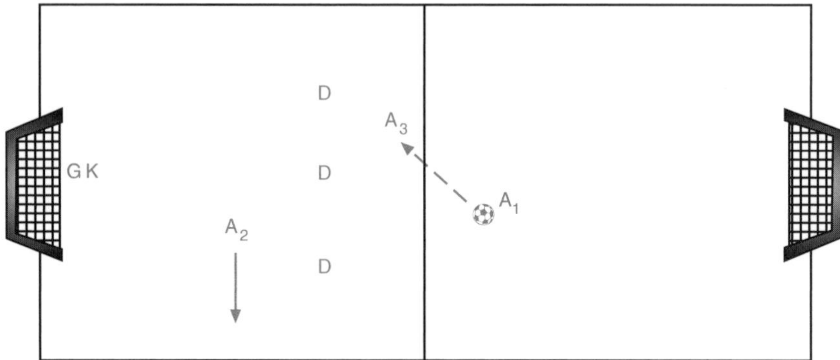

Figure 7.7 Legal offside position.

be ruled offside. When a player is offside, the opposing team receives an indirect free kick at the point of the infraction.

Goalkeeping

The following rules apply to goalkeepers:

- Goalkeepers may use their hands within the goal area to stop opponents' shots.
- Goalkeepers may use their hands to field a ball that has been headed or kneed to them deliberately by a teammate, but they may *not* use their hands to field a ball that has been kicked intentionally to them by a teammate.
- Goalkeepers may not pick up a throw-in from a teammate.
- Goalkeepers must release the ball within four steps, and they may not touch the ball again before another player touches it outside of the penalty area.

Scoring

Each time the entire ball crosses the goal line between the goalposts, the offensive team is awarded one goal. Scoring a goal is one of the tangible ways to measure personal performance. However, don't overemphasize goal scoring in assessing a player's contribution. Give equal attention to players who make assists, tackles, or saves, and who demonstrate leadership, sporting behavior, and effort.

Officiating

The referee is responsible for enforcing the rules, keeping the time and score, and issuing warnings and ejecting players and coaches. The referee signals the start and end of the game. The referee (or an assistant referee) indicates when and where a ball goes out of bounds and determines which team is awarded a goal kick, a throw-in, or a corner kick. Assistant referees also call offside plays and flag other violations that the referee misses. Figures 7.8 a-j show common officiating signals.

Figure 7.8 Officiating signals for *(a)* goal (points to center field for restart), *(b)* penalty kick (points to penalty area), *(c)* corner kick (points to corner area), *(d)* goal kick (points to goal area), *(e)* advantage or play on, *(f)* official's timeout, *(g)* offside, *(h)* indirect free kick, *(i)* direct free kick, and *(j)* caution or ejection.

Figure 7.8 *(continued)*

chapter 8

Tactics and Skills

As your athletes play games in practice, their experience in these games—and your subsequent discussions with them about their experience—will lead them to the tactics and skills they need to develop to succeed. In the games approach, teaching tactics and skills go hand in hand.

In this chapter we'll provide information for you for teaching your players team tactics and individual offensive and defensive skills. We'll also include suggestions for identifying and correcting common errors. Remember to use the IDEA approach to teaching skills—Introduce, Demonstrate, Explain the skill, and Attend to players practicing the skill. For a refresher on IDEA, see chapter 5. If you aren't familiar with soccer skills, rent or purchase a video to see the skills performed. You may also find advanced books on skills helpful.

We've provided information only about the basics of soccer in this book. As your players advance in their soccer skills, you'll need to advance your knowledge as a coach. You can do so by learning from your experiences, by watching and talking with more experienced coaches, and by studying advanced resources.

Team Tactics

The tactics you should teach players to use when their team has the ball are to support each other on the field by using the triangle method, to move continuously during play, to spread out the attack, and to pass and shoot often. Other team tactics include executing the give-and-go, setting up corner kicks, and defending during corner kicks.

Providing Support

Essential to any soccer team's success is how players support their teammates on the field. Teaching them the triangle concept is one way you can reinforce the need to spread out, provide support, and give the dribbler more options. The triangle concept is simply that players should try to maintain a triangle formation on the field, with the dribbler usually at the apex of the triangle (see figure 8.1). The triangle formation is

Figure 8.1 The triangle formation.

used in sports such as hockey and basketball, ones in which a fluid, dynamic interplay is required.

By maintaining a triangle, players will be able to spread out the defense and at the same time provide the player with the ball with more options.

To teach young players proper triangle positioning, use the easiest possible explanation. One method is to position players along the outer edges of the dribbler's field of vision. Players can find these outer edges by swinging both arms from behind the back around to the front until they are just visible.

In general, two or three teammates should provide support at one time; more will draw too many defenders and clog the attack. General guidelines for distance from the ball while providing support is 3 to 5 yards in close quarters and 8 to 10 yards if defenders are not challenging for possession (see figure 8.2).

Figure 8.2 Proper support distance from the ball.

Providing Support Game

TRAVELING LIGHT

Goal

To develop providing support

Description

Play 4v4, Team B with a goalkeeper. Set up a 20- × 60-yard area and divide it into three zones each 20 × 20 yards (see figure 8.3). Set up a goal 6 yards wide for younger players and 8 yards wide for older players, using two flags. The game starts with three attackers vs. one defender in zone 1. The attackers pass three times in zone 1; the player who receives the third pass and the player who passed it move to zone 2. Another attacker and another defender are waiting in zone 2, and the players repeat the same sequence used in zone 1. In zone 3,

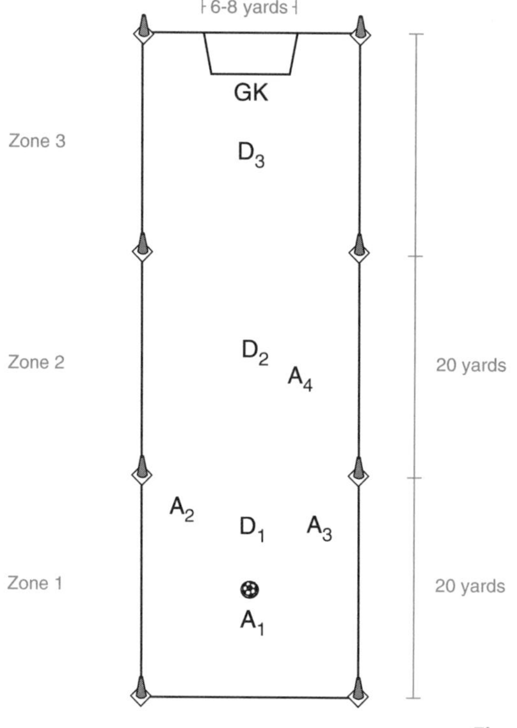

Figure 8.3 Setup for Traveling Light.

the three attacking players from zone 2 combine to try to beat a single defender and finish with a shot.

Award the attacking team a point for successfully passing through each zone. If the defenders tackle or intercept the ball, the attacking team receives no points, but the ball is returned to the attacking team so it can attempt the next zone. Rotate the offense and defense after the offense has gone through all three zones.

To make the game easier

- Increase the length and width of the field.
- Play 4v1 in each segment.

To make the game harder

- Decrease the length and width of the field.
- Play 3v2 in each segment.

Moving Continuously

Offensive players are easy to mark if they are inactive. Encourage your players to move continuously to an open area to receive passes. If teammates are not open, the dribbler should move the ball to an open area. This tactic will put pressure on the defense and probably cause one of the defensive players to leave his or her player, leaving one offensive player open for a pass. When a pass is made, the player to whom the pass was intended should come to meet the ball.

Error Detection and Correction for Receiving Passes

ERROR The receiver waits for a pass to arrive when a defender is in the area.

CORRECTION

1. Tell players to be aware of the pass, including its direction and velocity.
2. Instruct players to notice the position of defenders in relation to the path of the pass.
3. Insist that receivers move to meet the ball as quickly as possible (see figure 8.4) while still maintaining sufficient control to receive the pass.

Figure 8.4 Players should move to meet the ball as quickly as possible.

Pass Receiving Game

HOT POTATO

Goal

To develop receiving with the foot, thigh, or chest

Description

Play 3v3 with no goalkeepers in a 25- × 25-yard area (see figure 8.5). The focus is on controlling the ball; there are no goals to shoot at. Award 1 point for every pass received and controlled by the foot and 2 points each for every pass received and controlled by the thigh or chest. Keep track of each team's points.

To make the game easier

- Play 3v1 or 4v2.
- Increase the playing area to 30 × 30 yards.

To make the game harder

- Play 2v3 or 3v4.
- Decrease the playing area to 20 × 20 yards.

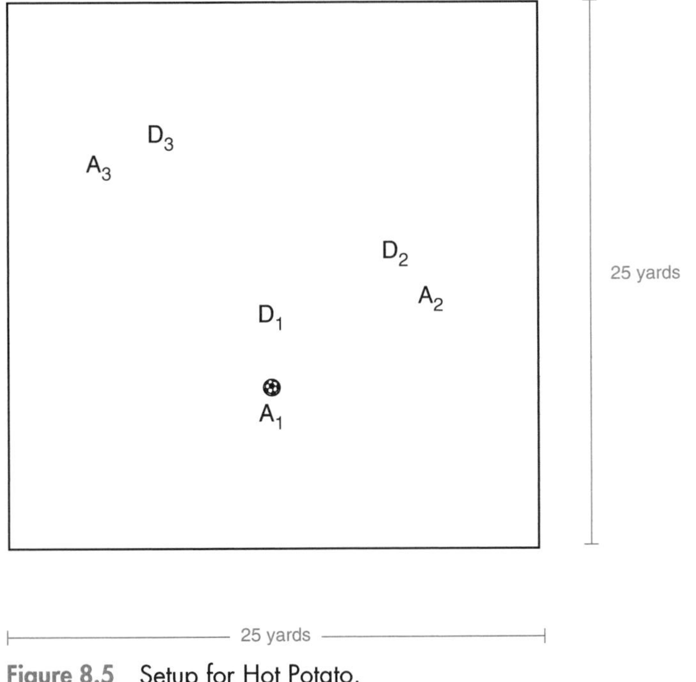

Figure 8.5 Setup for Hot Potato.

Spreading Out the Attack

Have your players keep distance between each other on the field. By spreading your offensive attack, your team will open up space for dribbling, passing, and scoring opportunities (see figure 8.6). Bunching together brings more defenders into position to intercept a pass or steal the ball. Also, when offensive players are too close together, more than one player can be guarded by only one defender.

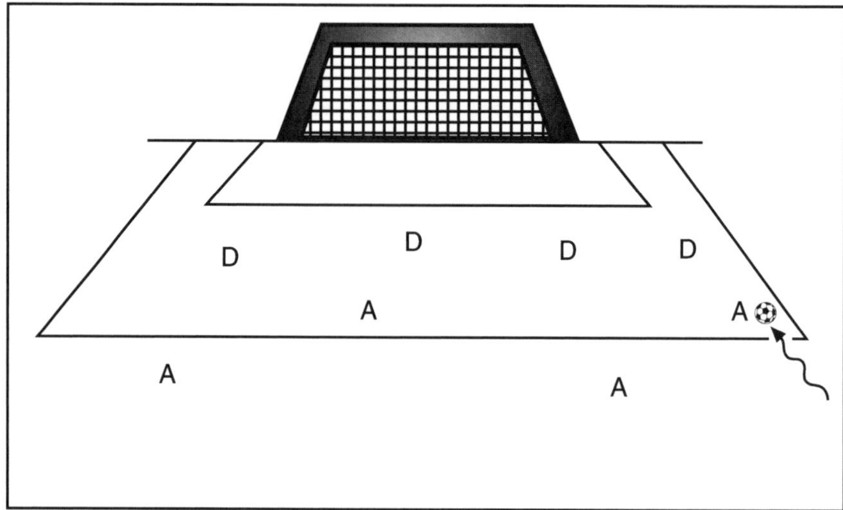

Figure 8.6 Correct offensive attack.

Error Detection and Correction for Offensive Attack

ERROR Offensive players position themselves in a straight line across the field.

CORRECTION

1. Get depth to the attack by having your players form two big "V"s on the offensive end of the field (see figure 8.7).
2. Tell players to be aware of their positions relative to offensive teammates and try to form triangles across the field.

Passing and Shooting Frequently

Quick, frequent passes require the defense to adjust constantly. Also, when defenders are out of position, it is easier to shoot the ball to the goal. The more shots on goal taken by your players, the greater your team's chances to score, but make sure they're good shots from reasonable distances and angles.

Executing the Give-and-Go

The give-and-go is the perfect tactic for two attackers to beat a single defender. The player with the ball dribbles at and commits the defending player to him or her, then passes to a nearby teammate (see figure 8.8a)

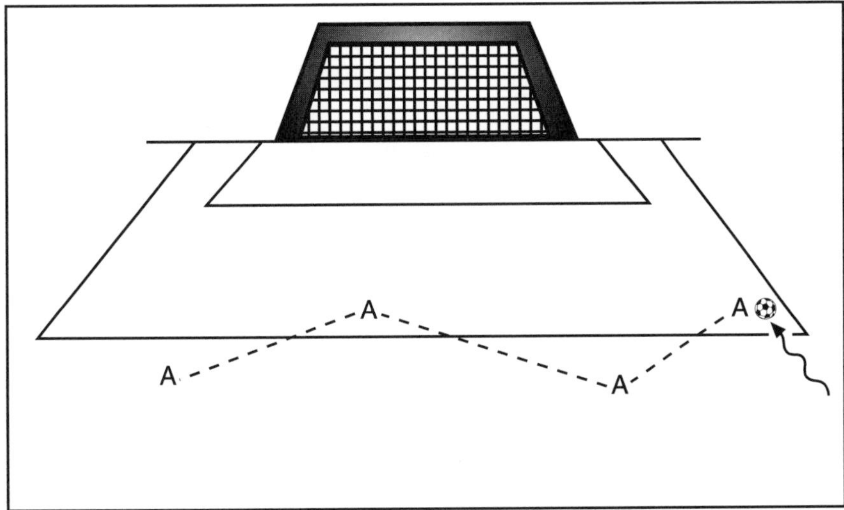

Figure 8.7 The V formation of an offensive attack.

before sprinting into the space behind the defender to collect a return pass (see figures 8.8 b and c). Note that to commit a defender, the attacker must get the defender to step forward to tackle the ball.

It is the first attacker's responsibility to get the defender to commit and then to successfully pass to the second attacker. It is the second

a

Figure 8.8 The give-and-go.

(continued)

b

c

Figure 8.8 *(continued)*

attacker's responsibility to be about three to four yards to the side of the defending player, at about a 45-degree angle from the first attacker. The second attacker executes a one-touch pass to the space behind the defender, and then sprints forward to support his or her teammate.

Give-and-Go Game

FRIEND OR FOE

Goal

To practice the give-and-go

Description

Play 4v4. Set up a 15- × 25-yard area (see figure 8.9) with two goals (6 yards wide for younger players; 8 yards wide for older players). Award each team points as follows:

- 3 points for a successful give-and-go
- 2 points for an unsuccessful give-and-go
- 1 point for a goal

Note: The give-and-go doesn't have to result in a goal to be successful—it just has to advance the ball downfield with the offense in control.

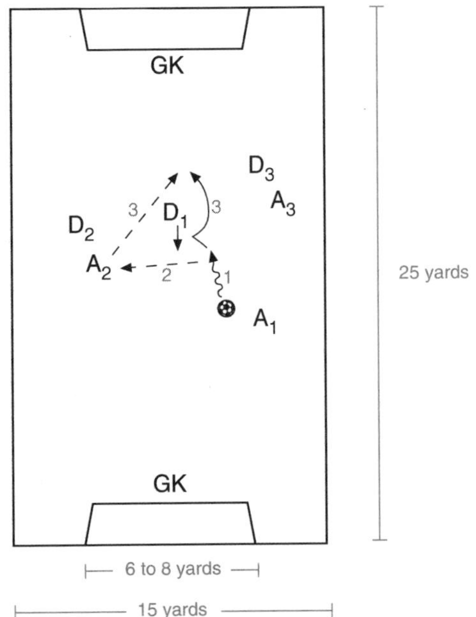

Figure 8.9 Setup for Friend or Foe.

(continued)

Friend or Foe *(continued)*

To make the game easier

- Play 5v3, 4v2, or 3v1.

To make the game harder

- Play 2v3 or 3v4.

Setting Up Corner Kicks

Corner kicks are executed most successfully when they are initiated by a kicker who can deliver an accurate ball to either the near-post area or far-post area (see figure 8.10). The best kicks are hard, low kicks across the face of the goal; these kicks should be in the air, not on the ground. Higher, softer kicks—and kicks on the ground—are easier to defend. Hard, low balls across the face of the goal present more opportunities for the attackers.

Defending During Corner Kicks

The most important areas to defend are the near-post area and the far-post area. Instruct your goalkeeper to try to win any ball within the goal area (i.e., about five to six yards in front of the goal line), but not beyond (see figure 8.11).

Figure 8.10 Corner kick.

Figure 8.11 The goalkeeper should attempt to win any ball within the goal area on a corner kick.

You can defend corner kicks either by using a zone defense, with the focus being on the near-post and far-post areas, or by marking player to player. You also can try a combination of the two, with some players assigned to cover the post areas and others assigned to individual attackers.

Corner Kicking Game

CORNER KICKING

Goal

To attack and defend at corner kicks

Description

Set up an area 20 yards long by 40 yards wide, with one goal (6 yards wide for younger players; 8 yards wide for older players; see figure 8.12). Play 4v4. Team A, on offense, gets four corner kicks (one for each player), attempting to score on each kick. Award points in this way:

- 2 points for a goal scored directly off a corner kick
- 1 point for a goal scored before the defense can control the ball

(continued)

Corner Kicking *(continued)*

Once everyone on Team A has had a chance to make a corner kick, Team A goes on defense, and Team B goes on offense. Repeat the sequence of kicks for each player.

To make the game easier

- Play 5v3 or 4v2.
- Don't allow the defense to touch the ball first, even if they are able to do so.

To make the game harder

- Play 4v5 or 3v5.
- Award points only for direct scoring directly off corner kicks.

Note: To focus on defense, award points only to the defense. Give a point for not allowing a score on a corner kick, and play 2v4, 3v5, or 4v6, depending on your players' proficiency.

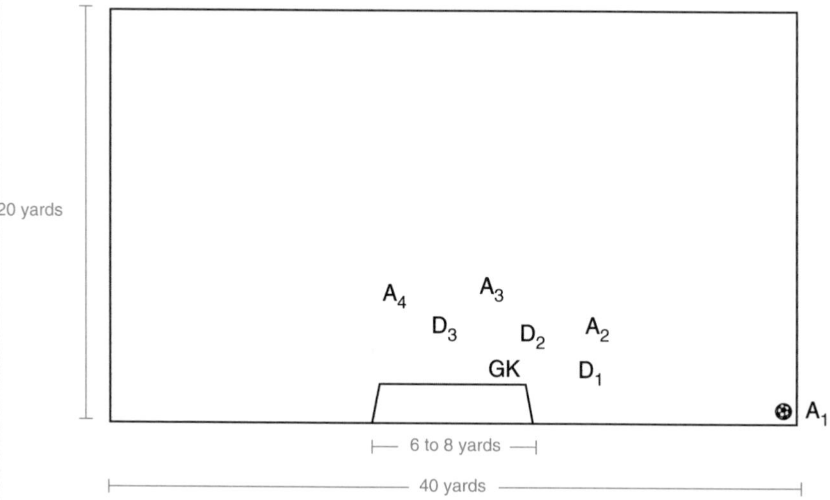

Figure 8.12 Setup for Corner Kicking.

Individual Offensive Skills

The offensive skills that you will want to help your players develop are dribbling, passing, receiving, heading, and shooting.

Dribbling

Dribbling is moving and controlling the ball using only the feet. Players should learn to dribble to move the ball down the field for a pass or shot, to keep the ball from the opposing team, and to change direction.

Players need to be able to use both the insides (see figure 8.13) and outsides (see figure 8.14) of their feet to dribble. To dribble with the inside of the foot, the player turns the foot out, then pushes the ball forward while moving. To dribble with the outside of the foot, the player turns the foot in, then pushes the ball slightly forward or to the side.

Players may have trouble dribbling at first. Have them start by walking and dribbling. Once they can do that, ask them to speed up their dribbling pace. Insist that they try to look up as they dribble and not down at the ball. If they always look down, they are likely to have the ball stolen by an opponent and are not likely to see a teammate who is open for a pass. Encourage players to use either foot to dribble—this will make it easier for them to protect the ball from opponents.

Figure 8.13 Dribbling with the inside of the foot.

Figure 8.14 Dribbling with the outside of the foot.

As your players improve, have them dribble against an opponent (see figure 8.15). Being marked (guarded) by a defender will require them to vary their speed, change direction, and shield the ball. Have them prepare for defensive pressure by practicing speeding up and slowing down as they dribble and by dribbling around towels or cones.

- Push the ball softly in the desired direction if you are dribbling close to defenders.
- Look up and watch for other players.
- Keep the ball close to your feet. If it is too far ahead, other players can steal it.
- Shield the ball from opponents.
- Run at a speed at which you can control the ball.
- If you are speed dribbling, push the ball out several feet ahead and sprint to the ball.

Figure 8.15 Player dribbling against opponent.

Error Detection and Correction for Dribbling

ERROR The ball gets too far away to keep possession.

CORRECTION

1. Keep the ball underneath the body, close to the feet (see figure 8.16).
2. Nudge the ball gently in different directions, never letting it get more than a stride's length away.
3. Determine whether the grass or ball requires adjustments. A very inflated ball or very short grass will cause the ball to roll faster and farther.

Figure 8.16 Keep the ball close to the feet, especially when being marked by a defender.

Dribbling Games

DRIBBLE ATTACK

Goal

To develop and encourage dribbling with both feet

Description

Play 3v3 in a 30- × 30-yard area (see figure 8.17). The offense gets a point whenever a player is able to dribble past his or her defender. The offense can pass to advance the ball, but they don't receive points for passing past a defender. As an option, you might give players an additional point for dribbling past a defender while using their "weak" foot.

To make the game easier

- Play 3v2 or 2v1.

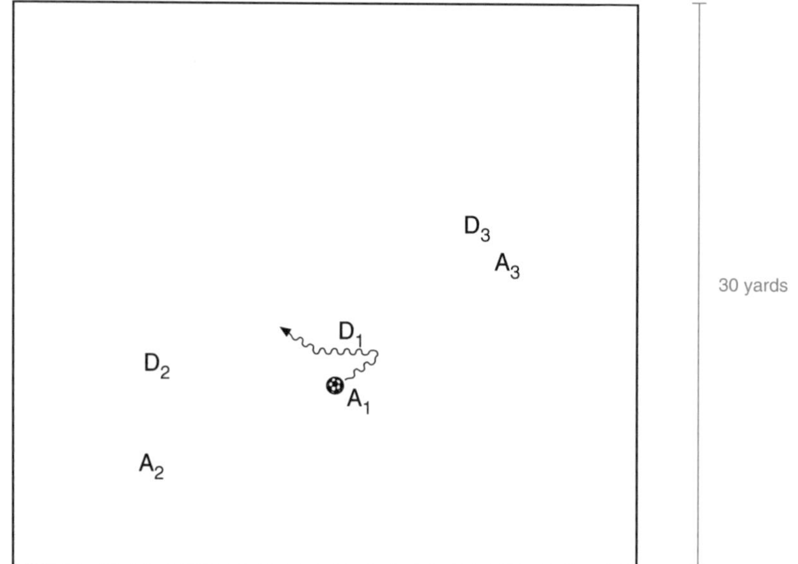

Figure 8.17 Dribble Attack.

To make the game harder

- Award points only for dribbling past a defender with the weak foot.

FOUR-GOAL MAYHEM

Goal

To encourage players to turn and change direction

Description

Play 4v4 within a 30- × 30-yard area marked off with cones. Each team has two goals to attack that are opposite each other and two different goals to defend. One team attacks goals A and B and defends goals C and D; the other attacks goals C and D and defends goals A and B. Each goal is 3 yards wide, and there are no goalkeepers (see figure 8.18). Points are scored by passing, shooting, or dribbling through the goals. Each time a point is scored, the coach restarts the

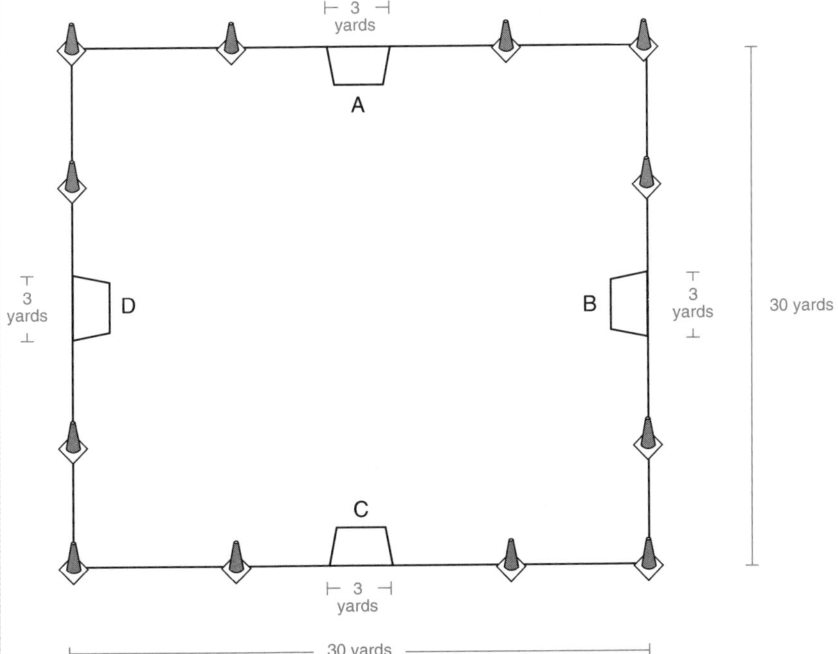

Figure 8.18 Setup for Four-Goal Mayhem.

(continued)

Four-Goal Mayhem *(continued)*

game by dropping the ball in the middle. When the ball goes out of play, restart the game with a throw-in.

To make the game easier

- Allow both teams to score on any goal.

To make the game harder

- Reduce the space to 20 × 20 yards to create more pressure to turn in tight spaces.
- Play 2v2, with four goalkeepers, in a 15- × 15-yard area.
- Increase space to 40 × 40 yards to play 6v6.

Passing

Passing is another essential skill, as it allows the team to maintain possession of the ball and create scoring opportunities. Passes should be short and crisp; long or slow passes are likely to be stolen by an opposing player. However, players should avoid using passes that are too hard and difficult to control.

Short Passes

Short passes should be kicked with the inside of the foot. Figure 8.19 shows the correct technique for short passes:

1. Plant the nonkicking foot alongside and near the ball (see figure 8.19a).
2. Square up the hips and shoulders to the teammate for whom the pass is intended and turn out the kicking foot (see figure 8.19b).
3. Swing the kicking foot straight at the center of the ball.
4. Follow through by swinging the kicking leg well beyond the point of impact with the ball, in the direction of the teammate to whom the ball is being passed (see figure 8.19c).

A *first-touch pass* is a pass that is made with the player's first touch of the ball. Such passes may be called upon when players are tightly marked or when they are about to receive a ball that is in danger of being taken by an opponent. Passing technique is essentially the same as described above, but less-skilled players will have more difficulty with first-touch passes because they have less control of the ball and aren't able to set up their passes better.

Figure 8.19 Proper technique for kicking short passes.

Short Passing Game

SHORT AND SHARP

Goal

To develop short passing technique

Description

Play 3v3, one team with a goalkeeper among its three players. Use cones to set up a 15- × 30-yard area with one goal (6 yards wide for younger players and 8 yards wide for older players). Divide it into two 15- × 15-yard zones (see figure 8.20). Play 3v1 in zone 1. The attackers must pass three times before moving into zone 2, where they will again play 3v1 and make three passes before shooting. If a

(continued)

Short and Sharp *(continued)*

defender wins the ball, the game restarts with a free pass between attackers. Defenders must stay in their zones.

One team remains on offense for five minutes, while the other team remains on defense; then flip-flop.

Award the offense 2 points for successfully passing in zone 1, 2 points for successfully passing in zone 2, and 1 point for a goal. "Successfully passing" means maintaining possession of the ball.

To make the game easier

- Play 4v1 in each zone.

To make the game harder

- Allow the defender in zone 1 to move to zone 2 once the ball is in zone 2.
- Play 3v2 or 4v2 in each zone.

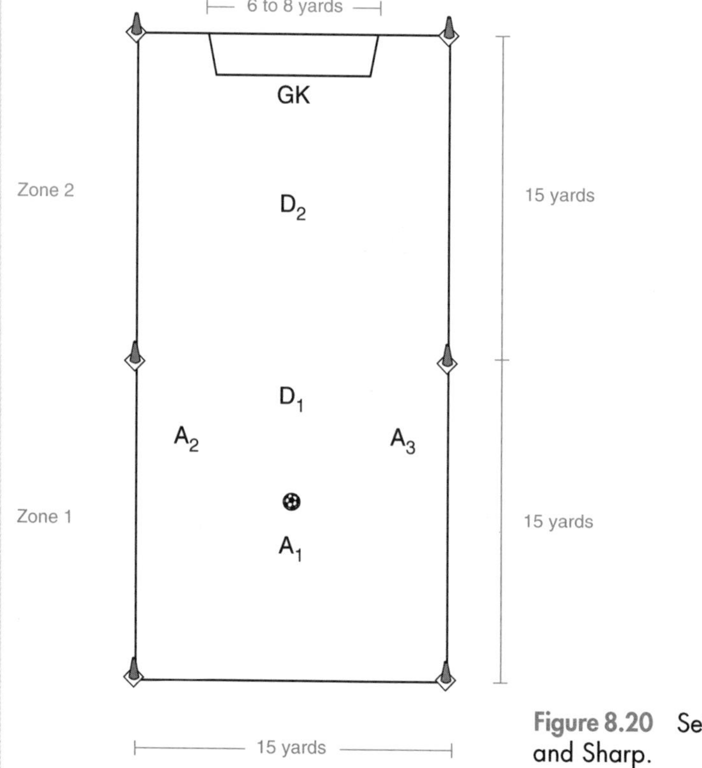

Figure 8.20 Setup for Short and Sharp.

Long Passes

Sometimes a game situation will call for a player to make a long pass to a teammate across the field. The best way to make a long pass is to loft the ball through the air using the top of the foot. This is the correct technique for lofting passes:

1. Plant the nonkicking foot slightly behind and to the side of the ball (see figure 8.21a).
2. Point the toes of the kicking foot down, and kick the ball with the shoelace area. Kick under the ball (see figure 8.21b).
3. Watch the kicking foot contact the bottom half of the ball and lift it off the ground (see figure 8.21c).

Figure 8.21 Proper technique for kicking long passes.

Error Detection and Correction for Passing

ERROR Passes are inaccurate.

CORRECTION

1. Plant the nonkicking foot beside the ball with the toes pointed toward the teammate who is to receive the pass.
2. Square your shoulders and hips to the receiver.
3. Keep the kicking foot firm throughout the kicking motion.
4. Follow through with the kicking foot.

Long Passing Game

THE LONG BOMB

Goal

To develop and encourage long passing techniques by getting the ball to the target player

Description

Play 4v4, with an additional two target players. Use cones to mark a 20- × 40-yard area (see figure 8.22). Create a 10-yard zone that separates the target players from the other players. The target players stand in the 10-yard zone waiting to receive passes. Players must pass to the target players from behind the 10-yard line. A team gets a point for getting the ball to its target player.

The game restarts with a free pass from the target player to a player from the scoring team. Tell the defenders to stand still while the free pass is made. Play then continues.

When the ball goes out of play, possession changes. Spread out balls around the perimeter, so play can resume quickly. The game restarts with a free pass in (defenders do not move during the free pass). Passes to target players cannot be made directly from a restart.

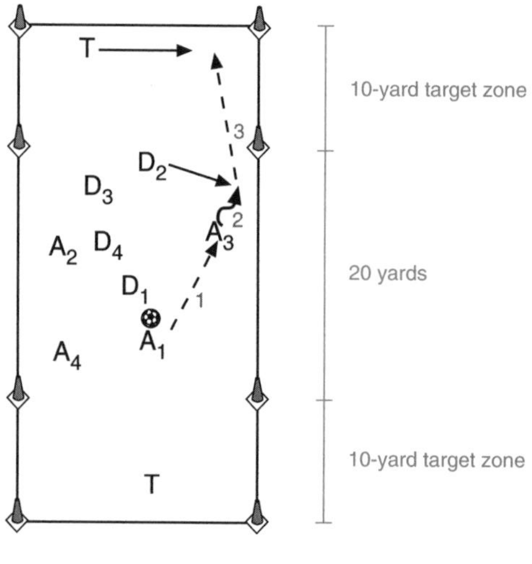

Figure 8.22 The Long Bomb.

To make the game easier

- Allow players to score points by lofting or driving the ball in to the target player.
- Reduce the field to 20 × 30 yards.

To make the game harder

- Give each player only two touches to play when he or she has possession.
- Increase the field size to 30 × 60 yards or play 5v5.

Receiving

In soccer, receiving and controlling a passed ball is called *receiving*. A player can receive the ball with just about any part of the body—the foot, the thigh, or the chest. Here are some key components in receiving:

1. Get in front of the ball.
2. Watch the ball.
3. Cushion the ball.
4. Keep the ball near the body.

At this level, you will be teaching players how to receive with the foot, the thigh, and the chest.

Receiving With the Foot

To receive the ball on or near the ground with the foot, the player should stand in front of the ball and extend a leg and foot out to meet it (see figure 8.23a). After the ball reaches the player's foot, he or she should pull the leg back to slow the ball and relax the foot when the ball makes contact (see figure 8.23b). This technique is called *cushioning* the ball. If a player does not cushion the ball, it will bounce away from the foot and the player will lose control. Receiving with the inside of the foot provides the most surface area and is best for inexperienced players. Eventually, players should learn how to receive with the outside and top of both feet. Note that players receiving with the top of the foot should also use the lower shin and front part of the ankle to cushion the ball.

Figure 8.23 Receiving with the foot.

Error Detection and Correction for Receiving With the Foot

ERROR Losing control of the ball off the foot (see figure 8.24).

CORRECTION

1. Contact the bottom and side of the ball with the inside of the foot—midway between the heel and toes.
2. Cushion the impact of the ball by dropping the foot as the ball contacts it.

Figure 8.24 Contacting the ball with the top of the foot can cause a player to lose control of the ball.

Receiving With the Thigh

Players can receive the ball in the air with a thigh in the following manner:

1. Stand in front of the ball and flex one knee (see figure 8.25a).
2. Raise a leg to have the thigh in line with the descent of the ball (see figure 8.25b).
3. Stop the ball, cushioning it by dropping the knee slightly as the ball touches the thigh (see figure 8.25c). This will help keep the ball in the player's vicinity.
4. Control the ball by trapping with the foot (see figure 8.25d).

Figure 8.25 Receiving with the thigh.

Error Detection and Correction for Receiving With the Thigh

ERROR The ball bounces up and out of control upon contact with the thigh (see figure 8.26).

CORRECTION

1. Raise your thigh into the proper receiving position before the ball arrives.
2. Lower your leg as the ball contacts your thigh.

ERROR The ball bounces forward and out of control upon contact with the thigh (see figure 8.27).

CORRECTION

1. Position your thigh parallel to the ground as the ball arrives.
2. Receive the ball on the midthigh, halfway between the knee and hip.

Figure 8.26 Neglecting to cushion the ball can cause the ball to bounce out of control.

Figure 8.27 Contacting the ball with the knee rather than the thigh can cause the ball to bounce out of control.

Receiving With the Chest

Players can also use the chest to receive the ball in the following manner:

1. Stand in the ball's line of flight, arms held up for balance and the chest pushed out to meet the ball (see figure 8.28a).
2. As the ball contacts the body, pull the chest back to cushion the ball (see figure 8.28b).
3. Kill the bounce by trapping with the foot.

Figure 8.28 Receiving the ball with the chest.

Error Detection and Correction for Receiving With the Chest

ERROR The ball bounces off your chest and out of your range of control.

CORRECTION

1. Receive the ball just right or left of center chest, where muscle and soft tissue provide an excellent receiving surface.
2. Draw your chest backward a few inches as the ball makes contact.

ERROR The ball skips off your chest, over your shoulder, and past you (see figure 8.29).

CORRECTION Don't arch your body back so far. Arch only a few inches from the vertical position as you receive the ball.

Figure 8.29 Arching the back too far can cause the ball to skip over the shoulder and out of control.

Heading

Your players can head the ball to clear it from an area of attack. The skill often is performed incorrectly, many times because coaches don't know the exact technique involved. (*Note:* Teach heading to 12- to 14-year-olds only.) Give your players these tips to help them learn how to head the ball:

- Be balanced and relaxed with the feet slightly apart. Pull the head and body back and move to the ball (see figure 8.30a).
- Keep the eyes open and mouth closed. Gaping jaws can cause players to bite their tongues.
- Thrust the body forward to meet the ball, hitting it with the forehead at the hairline (see figure 8.30b). Meet the ball; don't wait for it.
- Clench the neck muscles, keeping the neck firm while driving forward (see figure 8.30c).

Figure 8.30 Proper technique for heading the ball.

Heading Game

HEADS UP

Goal

To develop heading skills

Description

Play 3v3 in a 20- × 20-yard area (see figure 8.31). Team A is on offense and has no goalkeeper; Team B is on defense and has a goalkeeper. There is one goal (6 yards wide for younger players and 8 yards wide for older players). After six minutes the two teams rotate, and Team B is on offense.

The goal is to score goals. A goal scored "normally"—by kicking—is worth 1 point. A goal scored by heading is worth 2 points. The game is played normally during minutes 1, 3, and 5. During minutes 2, 4, and 6, call, "Heads up!" to indicate a minute of heading for the team on offense. During each minute, one specific player will be the header; he or she will receive tosses from a teammate and attempt to head the ball into the goal. During the "heading" time, the game will shrink to 2v1, and the team on offense can attempt as many headers as possible.

Rotate the header so each player gets a chance to practice heading.

To make the game easier

- Use a bigger goal.
- Use no goalie during the heading sessions.

To make the game harder

- Use a smaller goal.

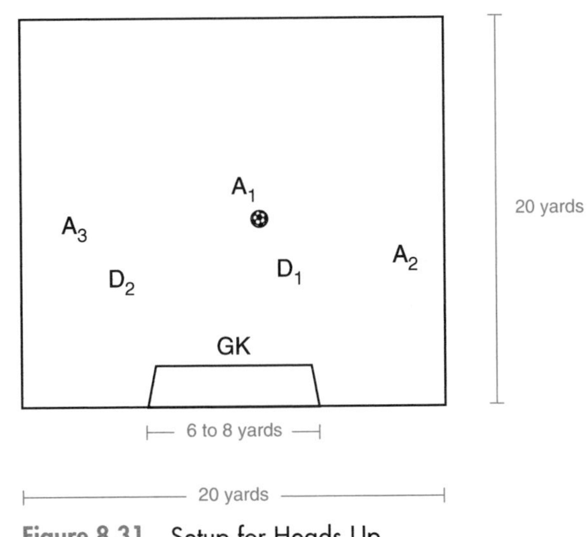

Figure 8.31 Setup for Heads Up.

Shooting

Every player likes to score goals, so your players will be highly motivated to learn proper shooting technique. Point out to them the similarities of shooting and passing; shots also come from the inside, top, and outside of the foot. Also mention some of these key differences between passing and shooting:

- *Length*—Shots often must travel a greater distance than passes because defenders work to keep offensive players away from the goal.
- *Speed*—Shooters frequently kick the ball harder than passers do so the goalie can't react to stop the shot. Unlike the passer, the shooter doesn't need to be concerned about whether a teammate can control the kick.
- *Purpose*—Shots are taken for one reason: to score a goal. However, players pass the ball for many different reasons, such as to get a better shot or to keep the ball away from the defense.

Players should use the instep for shooting either a stationary or rolling ball. The mechanics are as follows:

- Approach the ball from behind and at a slight angle (see figure 8.32a).
- Take a long step (which acts to draw your kicking leg back) and plant your balance foot beside the ball with the knee of your balance leg slightly flexed (see figure 8.32b).

(continued)

Figure 8.32 Proper technique for shooting the ball.

c

d

Figure 8.32 *(continued)*

- Keep your head steady and focus on the ball.
- Extend your kicking foot; the knee of your kicking leg should be directly over the ball (see figure 8.32c).
- Whip your leg straight and contact the center of the ball with your instep; keep your foot firm and pointed down as it strikes the ball (see figure 8.32d).
- Keep your shoulders and hips square to the target.
- Follow through completely for maximum power.

Instruct your players to shoot often. Nothing puts greater pressure on the defense than shots on goal. More accurate shooters should aim away from the goalie and toward corners of the goal; less accurate shooters can attempt to hit the corners also but might consider at times using the whole goal as the target.

Error Detection and Correction for Shooting

ERROR Shots are slow and inaccurate (see figure 8.33).

CORRECTION

1. Square shoulders and hips to the goal.
2. Keep the kicking leg cocked until the nonkicking foot is firmly planted beside the ball.
3. Strike the ball cleanly with the foot, keeping the toe down.
4. Watch the ball as it leaves the kicking foot.
5. Follow through completely, keeping the kicking leg pointing toward the goal well beyond the point of impact.

Figure 8.33 Kicking with the toes pointed up can cause shots to be inaccurate.

Shooting Games

STRIKE FORCE

Goal

To develop shooting ability

Description

Play 5v5, with one goalkeeper on each side (see figure 8.34). Use cones to set up a 25- × 44-yard area, with two goals (6 yards wide for younger players and 8 yards wide for older ones). Within the area, mark two 25- × 18-yard zones (1 and 2), with a neutral zone of 8 yards in between into which shooters can enter to shoot without being challenged. The game starts with the zone 1 goalkeeper's distributing the ball to one of his or her team's players. That player dribbles or passes to another player to get the ball into the neutral zone. Allow only one defender in zone 1; have the other three in zone 2.

Once an attacker has the ball in the neutral zone, he or she shoots from there, but none of the other attackers from zone 1 can cross into the neutral zone. The attacking team has a lone "sniper" in zone 2. If the ball is intercepted by the defenders, the sniper can steal the ball back and shoot it. When the sniper's own team shoots, the sniper can try to shoot rebounds or deflections from the goalkeeper or defenders into the goal.

Play restarts when a goalie controls and distributes the ball to a teammate. All players stay in their zones except the attacker, who goes to the neutral zone to shoot.

To make the game easier

- Defenders cannot intercept shots; shots are allowed to go through to the goalie.
- Shorten the length of the field.

To make the game harder

- Lengthen the field.
- Remove the neutral zone. Make a halfway line and restrict teams to shooting only from their own halves. The sniper cannot shoot directly into the goal but can pass the ball back to teammates.

(continued)

Strike Force *(continued)*

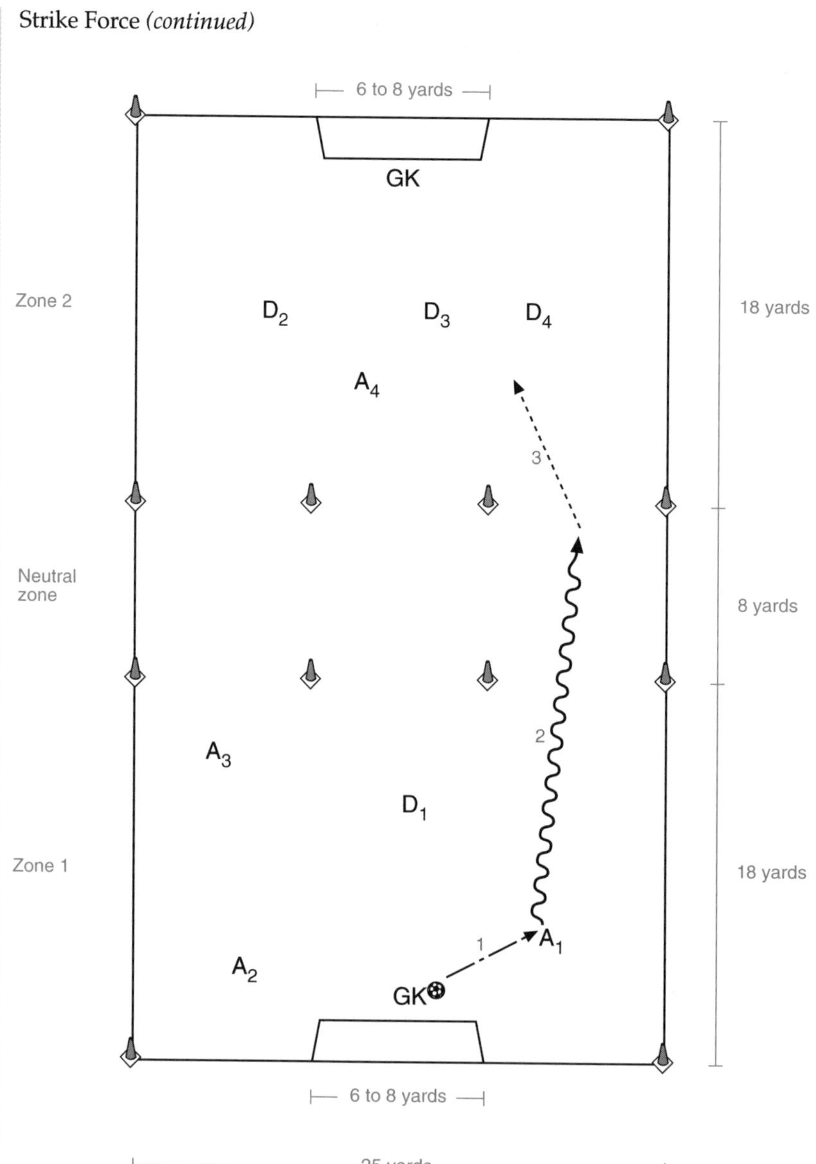

Figure 8.34 Strike Force.

SHOOTING STARS

Goal

To develop shooting ability

Description

Play 3v4 with one goalie. Set up a 20- × 30-yard area with one goal (6 yards wide for younger players and 8 yards wide for older ones; see figure 8.35). Award 1 point for each shot attempted and 2 points for each goal. After the teams play three minutes, have them switch sides.

To make the game easier

- Play 4v3 or 5v3.

To make the game harder

- Play 2v4 or 3v5.

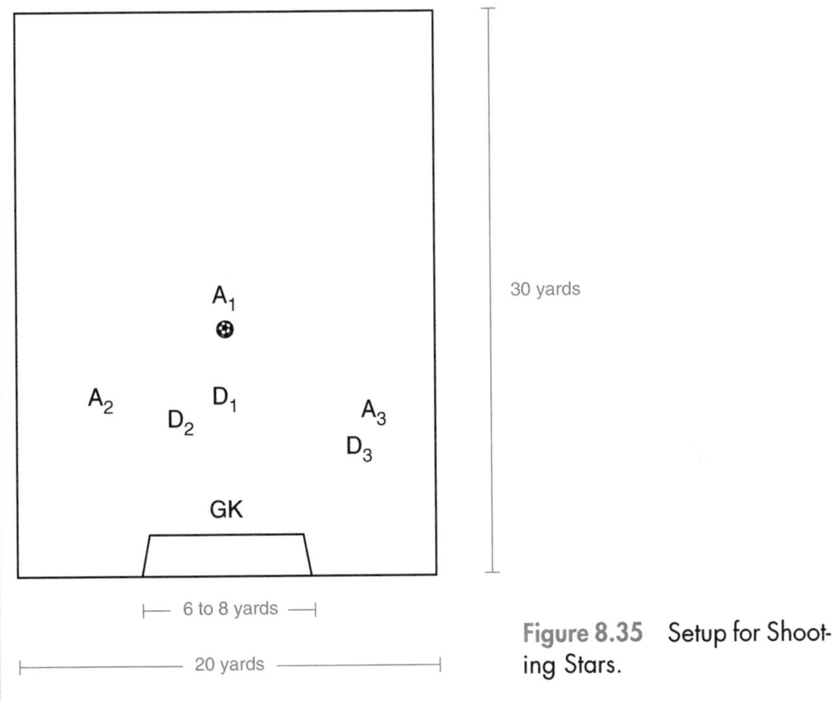

Figure 8.35 Setup for Shooting Stars.

Now that we've reviewed the main individual offensive skills, let's move on to the defensive skills.

Individual Defensive Skills

The three defensive skills your players will need to learn are marking, tackling, and goalkeeping.

Marking

Marking is guarding offensive players to prevent them from scoring. Defenders should try to mark the offensive player to whom they are assigned, staying near that player and between that player and the goal (this is called being "goal-side"). From this position, defensive players will be able to gain possession of the ball off the dribble and intercept passes. Marking is used to slow down an opponent and to allow teammates to recover to their positions.

Get your players to notice opponents' habits, such as using only one leg to dribble, pass, or shoot. Then they'll be able to overplay the offensive players to whom they are assigned and perhaps block or gain possession of the ball frequently.

Teach your players to get close to the player they are marking when that player has the ball. The closer a defender is to the player with the ball, the more difficult it is for that player to pass and shoot (see figure 8.36).

Figure 8.36 Shooting is difficult when a defender is close.

Thus, your players will have a better chance of stealing or blocking the ball when the opponent passes or shoots. Remind your players that they must first be between the opponent with the ball and the goal to reduce the shooting angle (see figure 8.37).

Figure 8.37 A defender should be between the player with the ball and the goal to reduce the shooting angle.

Error Detection and Correction for Marking

ERROR The offensive player gets by with the dribble.

CORRECTION

1. Maintain ready position.
2. Calculate and respect the dribbler's speed and ability, and adjust marking distance accordingly (see figure 8.38a).
3. Watch the ball.
4. Attempt tackles off the ball only when the ball is off the dribbler's foot (see figure 8.38b).

Figure 8.38 Proper technique for marking and attempting a tackle off the ball.

Marking Game

MONKEY ON THEIR BACKS

Goal

To develop marking skills

Description

Play 2v2 or 3v3. Set up a 15- × 30-yard area (see figure 8.39). The goal is to stay between the attacker with the ball and the defender's "goal" (however, there is no actual goal, and no shots will be taken; assign end lines to defend for each team). Only the *defense* can earn points. Give 1 point when an attacker cannot advance the ball, either by passing or dribbling, past his or her defender. (Award the point when the attacker is forced to pass back to a teammate.) Give 2 points if the ball is intercepted or otherwise taken away.

To make the game easier

- Allow the offensive team more time.
- Shorten the number of yards needed to score points.

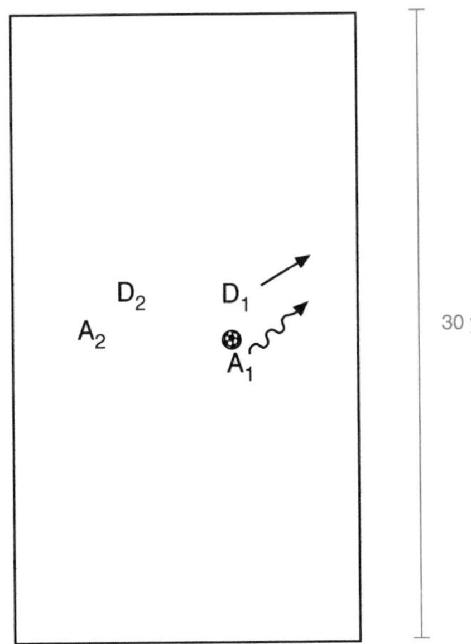

Figure 8.39 Monkey on Their Backs.

(continued)

Monkey on Their Backs *(continued)*

To make the game harder

- Allow the offensive team less time.
- Lengthen the number of yards needed to score points.

Tackling

Taking the ball from an offensive player is called *tackling*. Players should not be afraid to attempt to take the ball when they have a good opportunity, such as when the dribbler pushes the ball too far ahead. Defenders should, however, be prepared to reestablish position if they are unsuccessful in their take-away attempts.

Teach players to *time* their tackles; ideally, they should step in when the attacker temporarily loses control of the ball. Lunging at the ball—or "diving in"—is a dangerous tactic to teach. A good dribbler will usually go around a defender who lunges at the ball with no trouble (see figure 8.40). When positioning to make a tackle, the defender should approach the dribbler in a sideways position. If this technique is followed, the attacker cannot push the ball between the defender's legs. And remember, tell your players to go for the ball—not the opponent (see figure 8.41).

Following are instructions for two types of tackles: the block tackle and the poke tackle.

Figure 8.40 The dribbler can go around the defender if that defender lunges at the ball.

Figure 8.41 Defenders should go for the ball—not the opponent.

Block Tackle

Players should use a block tackle when an opponent is dribbling directly at them. Instruct them to quickly close the distance to the dribbler. As they do so, they should position their feet in a staggered stance, with one foot slightly ahead of the other, and get in a slightly crouched stance (see figure 8.42a). This will help them to be in position to react quickly to the dribbler's move.

They should tackle the ball by blocking it with the inside surface of the foot. Tell them to position the foot sideways and keep it firm as they drive it into the ball (see figure 8.42b). Remind them to play the ball, not the opponent, when tackling.

Figure 8.42 Proper technique for a block tackle.

Poke Tackle

Tell your players to use a poke tackle when they are approaching an opponent from the side or from slightly behind (see figure 8.43a). As they near the dribbler they should reach in with a leg, extending the foot, and poke the ball away with their toes (see figure 8.43b). Again, remind them to play the ball, not the opponent.

Figure 8.43 Proper technique for a poke tackle.

Error Detection and Correction for Tackling

ERROR The leg is overextended in attempting a tackle (see figure 8.44).

CORRECTION

1. Mark the dribbler as closely as possible and look for an opportunity to take possession of the ball.
2. If the dribbler is careless or unskilled, take advantage by tackling the ball.
3. Gain position by planting the nonkicking leg near the ball (see figure 8.45a). Then use a short, firm kick with the other leg to knock the ball away from the opponent (see figure 8.45b).

Figure 8.44 Overextending the leg while attempting a tackle can allow the dribbler to get by with the ball.

a b

Figure 8.45 Proper technique for attempting a tackle.

Tackling Games

THE DUEL

Goal

To develop tackling techniques

Description

Play 2v2 in a 15- × 20-yard area with two goals made using flags placed 5 yards apart (see figure 8.46). Set cones on each sideline, 4 yards away from each end line, to create two 4-yard shooting zones. Begin play at midfield.

The two defenders try to tackle the ball while the two offensive players try to move the ball down the field, and, once inside the 4-yard shooting zone, they can shoot on goal. If a goal is scored, the opposing team gets the ball and begins at its own end line.

For any ball that is tackled, give 2 points. If the ball leaves the field and is awarded to the defensive team, give 1 point.

To make the game easier

- Reduce the length of the field.
- Play 2v3.

To make the game harder

- Use two additional cones to create a dividing line halfway down the field, and require the defender to tackle in the opponent's half of the field only.
- Use two additional cones to create a dividing line halfway down the field. Allow the attacker to pass back to a teammate to relieve pressure from the defender, and require the defender to stay at the halfway line until the attacker gets the ball back from the teammate.

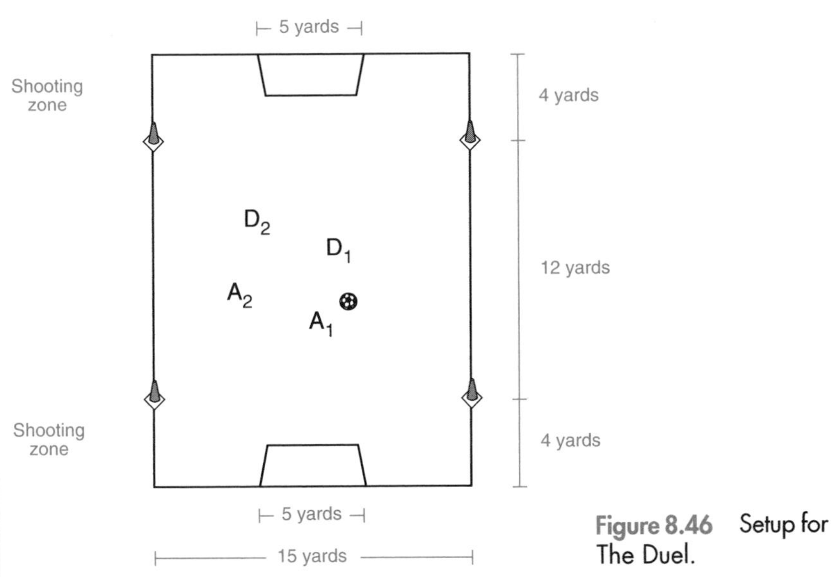

Figure 8.46 Setup for The Duel.

CRUNCH TIME

Goal

To develop block- and poke-tackling techniques

Description

Play 2v4, 3v5, or some other lopsided game with more players on the defensive side. Set up an area 15 × 30 yards with two goals (6 yards wide for younger players and 8 yards wide for older ones; see figure 8.47). Award a point for each block or poke tackle the defense

(continued)

Crunch Time *(continued)*

makes. After the defense makes a tackle, they return the ball to the offense. After five minutes, have the teams switch sides.

To make the game easier

- Decrease the size of the field.
- Add a defender.

To make the game harder

- Increase the size of the field.
- Add another offensive player.

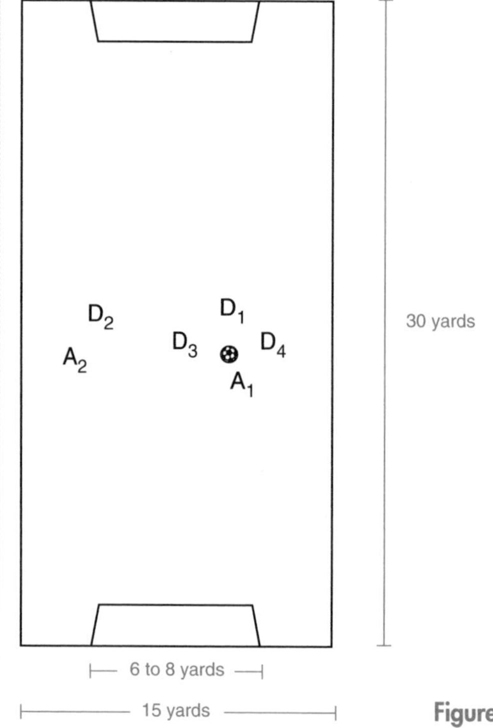

Figure 8.47 Setup for Crunch Time.

Goalkeeping

Playing goalie is fun and challenging. The goalkeeper must be alert and watch the ball at all times. As the last line of defense to prevent a goal, the goalkeeper has the greatest individual defensive responsibility on the team.

When an opponent has the ball within shooting distance of the goal, a goalkeeper should assume the ready position (see figure 8.48):

- shoulders squared to the ball with feet about shoulder-width apart;
- head and upper body erect and knees slightly flexed;
- hands at waist level with palms forward and fingers pointing upward; and
- head steady and eyes focused on the ball.

Figure 8.48 Ready position for goalkeepers.

From the ready position, goalies are ready to stop a shot. You should teach goalies how to

- narrow the shooting angle;
- gather balls on the ground;
- gather balls in the air;
- dive to save shots;
- collapse on the ball; and
- distribute the ball.

Narrow the Shooting Angle

A fundamental skill for goalkeepers is to narrow the shooting angle as an opponent is getting in position to shoot. Goalies should come off the

Figure 8.49 By coming off the goal line toward the ball, the goalkeeper reduces the shooting angle.

goal line toward the ball (see figure 8.49). This cuts down on the amount of goal that is accessible to the shooter.

Gathering Ground Balls

From the ready position, goalies should stop shots on the ground through these techniques:

- Quickly shuffle sideways to a position between the ball and the goal.
- Keep your legs straight, with your feet a few inches apart, and bend forward at the waist as the ball arrives (see figure 8.50a).
- Reach your arms down with your palms forward and slightly cupped.
- Allow the ball to roll up onto your wrists and forearms (see figure 8.50b).
- Return to an upright position, clutching the ball tightly to your chest (see figure 8.50c).

Figure 8.50 Proper technique for gathering ground balls.

Error Detection and Correction for Gathering Ground Balls

ERROR The ball rolls through your hands, between your legs, and into the goal.

CORRECTION Keep your feet only a few inches apart. If the ball slips through your hands, it will rebound off your legs.

ERROR The ball rebounds off your hands into the area in front of the goal (see figure 8.51).

CORRECTION Allow the ball to roll up onto your wrists and forearms, then use a scoop-like motion of your arms as you return to an upright position and clutch the ball to your chest.

Figure 8.51 Stiff wrists and forearms can cause the ball to rebound off the goalkeeper's hands.

Gathering Air Balls

For a ball that arrives between a goalkeeper's ankles and waist, the proper gathering technique is as follows:

- As the ball arrives, bend forward at the waist (see figure 8.52a).
- Extend arms down with palms facing forward.
- Receive the ball on the wrists and forearms, and secure it against your chest (see figure 8.52b).
- For waist-height balls, jump backward a few inches to absorb the impact.

a

b

Figure 8.52 Proper technique for gathering air balls.

For a ball that arrives chest- or head-high, goalkeepers should use this gathering technique:

- As the ball arrives, position your hands in the diamond position, with fingers spread and thumbs almost touching (see figure 8.53a).
- Extend your arms, slightly flexed at the elbows, toward the ball.
- Catch the ball with your fingertips (see figure 8.53b).
- Withdraw your arms to cushion the impact and secure the ball to your chest (see figure 8.53c).

Figure 8.53 Proper technique for gathering chest- or head-high balls.

For a ball that is lofted high in the air, the gathering technique is as follows:

- Move toward the ball and use a one-legged takeoff to generate maximum upward momentum (see figure 8.54a).
- Bend the front leg for protection.
- Extend your arms overhead and try to catch the ball at the highest point possible (see figure 8.54b).
- Secure the ball to your chest before you land (see figure 8.54c).

Figure 8.54 Proper technique for gathering high lofts.

Error Detection and Correction for Gathering Air Balls

ERROR You fail to hold the ball.

CORRECTION

1. Receive the ball on your wrists and forearms, then clutch it to your chest (see figure 8.55).
2. For chest- or head-high balls, use your hands to form the diamond position. Your thumbs and forefingers should almost touch behind the ball as you receive it (see figure 8.56).

ERROR The ball rebounds off you and out of your control.

CORRECTION

1. Jump back a few inches as the ball arrives, to absorb its impact.
2. For chest- or head-high balls, receive the ball on your fingertips, not on your palms (see figure 8.57). Flex your elbows and withdraw your arms as the ball arrives, to soften its impact.

ERROR On high-lofted balls, the ball goes over your head and into the goal.

CORRECTION

1. Judge the ball's path and move toward the oncoming ball.
2. Jump at the last possible moment, using a one-legged takeoff.
3. Receive the ball at the highest point of your jump.

Figure 8.55 Clutch ball to chest after gathering air balls.

Figure 8.56 Diamond position for receiving chest- or head-high balls.

Figure 8.57 To gather chest- or head-high balls, receive the ball on your fingertips.

Diving to Save Shots

Sometimes your goalkeepers will have to dive to save a shot. Here is the proper technique to do so:

- Step with the foot nearest the ball in the direction you are going to dive.

- Push off that foot to begin your dive (e.g., push off your right foot to dive to the right; see figure 8.58a).
- Extend your arms and hands toward the ball (see figure 8.58b).
- Position your hands in a sideways "W" and receive the ball on your fingertips and palms (see figure 8.58c).
- Place your lower hand behind the ball with elbow tucked to your side.
- Pin the ball to the ground with your upper hand (see figure 8.58d).
- Contact the ground with your side, not your stomach.

(continued)

Figure 8.58 Proper technique for diving to save shots.

c

d

Figure 8.58 *(continued)*

Collapsing on the Ball

Goalkeepers will at times have to collapse on a ball to secure it in tight quarters. As they secure the ball, they should collapse on their side, bringing the ball in and the top leg up in a fetal position (see figure 8.59). Instruct your goalies not to lie on their backs, but to stay on the side.

Figure 8.59 Goalkeeper in the fetal position to secure the ball.

Distributing the Ball

Goalies have three choices in distributing the ball to a teammate after making a save: rolling it, throwing it, or kicking it. The goalie must release the ball within four steps.

Rolling the Ball. Rolling the ball is good for distances of 10 to 15 yards or less. The motion is similar to that used when bowling. Goalies should cup the ball in the palm of the hand, step toward their target with the opposite foot, and release with a bowling-type motion (see figure 8.60). They should release the ball at ground level so it doesn't bounce.

Figure 8.60 Distribute the ball by rolling.

Throwing the Ball. To get greater distance, goalies can throw the ball, using an overhand motion similar to throwing a baseball, or a straight-arm overhand or three-quarter motion, similar to throwing a javelin. Goalies should hold the ball in the palm of the hand (see figure 8.61), step toward the target, and use a three-quarter or overhand throwing motion.

Kicking the Ball. Although kicking is less accurate than throwing, it can send the ball quickly into the opponent's end of the field. Goalies can use a *full volley punt* by holding the ball in the palm of the hand opposite the kicking foot, extending the arm so the ball is at waist level. They should step forward with the nonkicking foot, release the ball, and kick it with the instep, keeping their shoulders and hips square to the target (see figure 8.62). A *dropkick* is similar to a full volley punt, but the ball is dropped and is kicked immediately after it contacts the ground (see figure 8.63). The flight of a dropkicked ball is generally lower than that of a full volley punt, making it a better choice on a blustery day.

Figure 8.61 Distribute the ball by throwing.

Figure 8.62 Proper technique for a full volley punt.

Figure 8.63 Proper technique for a dropkick.

Error Detection and Correction for Distributing the Ball

ERROR The ball bounces toward the target when it is rolled.

CORRECTION Release the ball smoothly at ground level (see figure 8.64).

ERROR Your throw lacks accuracy or distance.

CORRECTION Step toward the target and use a complete follow-through motion.

ERROR Your kick lacks accuracy.

CORRECTION

1. Step toward the target with your nonkicking foot.
2. Square your shoulders and hips to the target.
3. Contact the center of the ball with the full instep (see figure 8.65).

ERROR Your kick lacks distance.

CORRECTION

1. Keep your foot firmly planted and kick through the point of contact, using your instep.
2. Swing your kicking foot waist high or higher (see figure 8.66).

Figure 8.64 Release the ball at ground level to keep the ball from bouncing toward the target.

Figure 8.65 Contact the center of the ball with the instep to ensure accuracy.

Figure 8.66 Swing the kicking foot at least waist high to add distance to the kick.

Goalkeeping Games

NARROW ENOUGH?

Goal

To develop the goalkeeper's ability to narrow the shooting angle

Description

Play 3v1: three offensive players against a goalkeeper. Set up a goal, using two flags (6 yards apart for younger players and 8 yards apart for older ones; see figure 8.67). The three offensive players pass among each other, attempting to score. The object is to try to shoot from the side, making the goalie narrow the angle to stop the shot. Give the offense 1 point for a goal scored head-on and 2 points for a goal scored from either side. Give the goalie a point for every shot stopped. After

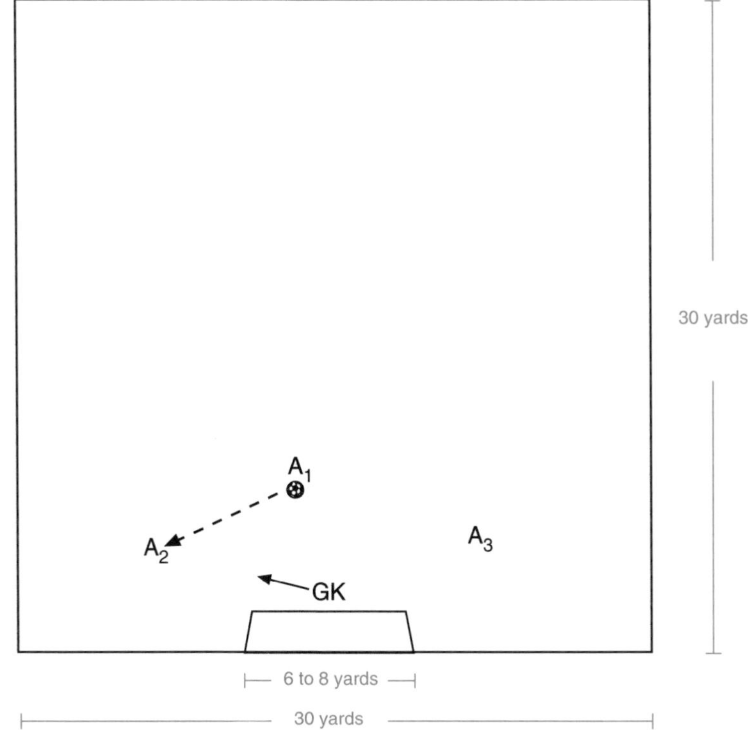

Figure 8.67 Narrow Enough?

(continued)

Narrow Enough? *(continued)*

five shots, rotate goalies; continue rotating until every player has played goalie.

To make the game easier

- Call out the side for the shot to come from.
- Increase the shooting distance.
- Use a smaller goal.

To make the game harder

- Reduce the shooting distance.
- Use a bigger goal.
- Add a player who tries to score goals from rebounds if the goalkeeper fails to deal with the shot effectively.

KEEPER WARS

Goal

To develop and encourage the basic diving technique for goalkeepers

Description

This game is for two players. Use cones to mark a 15- × 20-yard area, with one goal (use adjustable goals or four flags) that is 5 feet high (6 yards wide for younger players and 8 yards wide for older players; see figure 8.68). (If you use flags for the goal, set them up so they are 5 feet high.) The low goals force low shots and diving saves.

Place a goalkeeper in the goal and have the other player shoot at the goal. Give the goalie five tries to dive and save. (Encourage the goalkeeper to land on his or her side and to lead with the hands to make the save.) Award a point for each successful dive and save. Have the shooter redo any shots that don't require dives. Rotate the goalie and the shooter after five legitimate save attempts, and rotate the players through each role three times. Each player will attempt to save 15 shots, so "15" is a perfect score.

To make the game easier

- Reduce the width of the goal.
- Require longer shots.

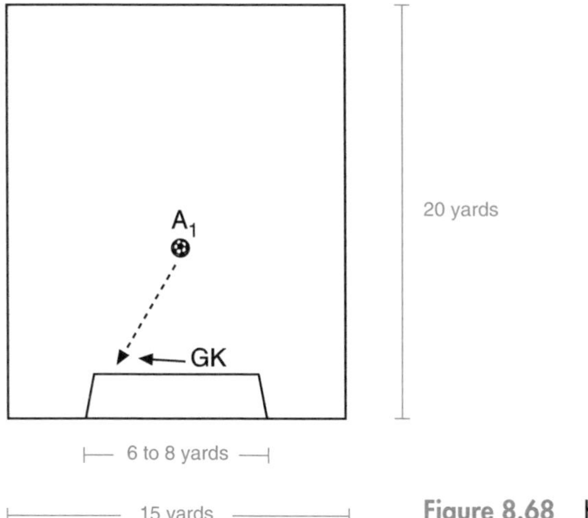

Figure 8.68 Keeper Wars.

To make the game harder

- Increase the width of the goal.
- Add a player who tries to score goals from rebounds if the goalkeeper fails to deal with the shot effectively.

Note: You can adapt this game to focus on goalkeepers gathering air balls, too, without diving for them.

BOWLING BALLS

Goal

To develop the ability to distribute the ball by rolling it

Description

Play 2v3. Use cones to set up a 20- × 20-yard area, and create one goal, 4 yards wide, using two flags (see figure 8.69). The two offensive players attack the goal; after the goalie saves a shot, he or she rolls the ball to a teammate. Give a point for each ball successfully rolled (one that is controlled by one of the goalie's teammates). Rotate goalies after three attempts at rolling the ball.

(continued)

Bowling Balls *(continued)*

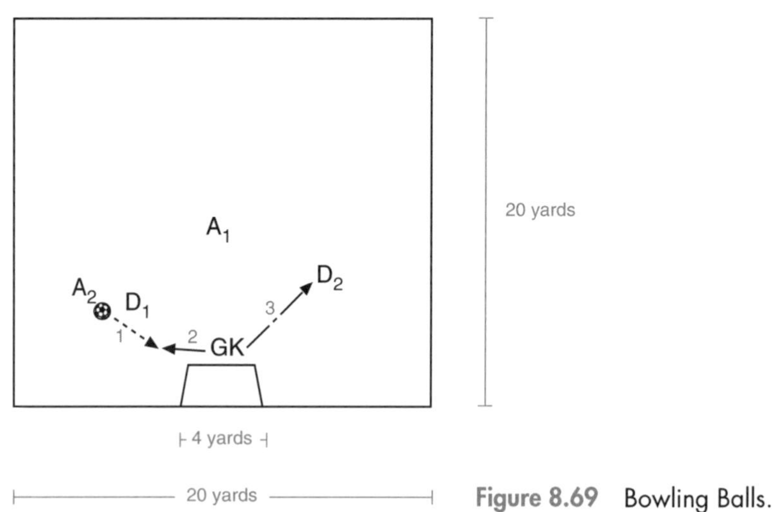

Figure 8.69 Bowling Balls.

To make the game easier

- Play 1v3 or 2v4.

To make the game harder

- Play 3v3.

ON THE MONEY

Goal

To develop the ability to distribute the ball by throwing it

Description

Play 3v3 in a 20- × 30-yard area with one goal (6 yards wide for younger players and 8 yards wide for older players; see figure 8.70). Team A is on offense for five minutes; instruct players to shoot as often as possible. Team B is on defense. The teams switch after five minutes, placing Team B on offense for the next five minutes.

The team on offense gets a point for each goal they score and for each ball distributed by the goalie that they can gain possession of before the goalie's teammates can. The defense gets a point each time the goalie successfully distributes the ball by throwing it to a teammate who can control the ball. Once the ball is distributed, begin play again with the ball going back to the offense.

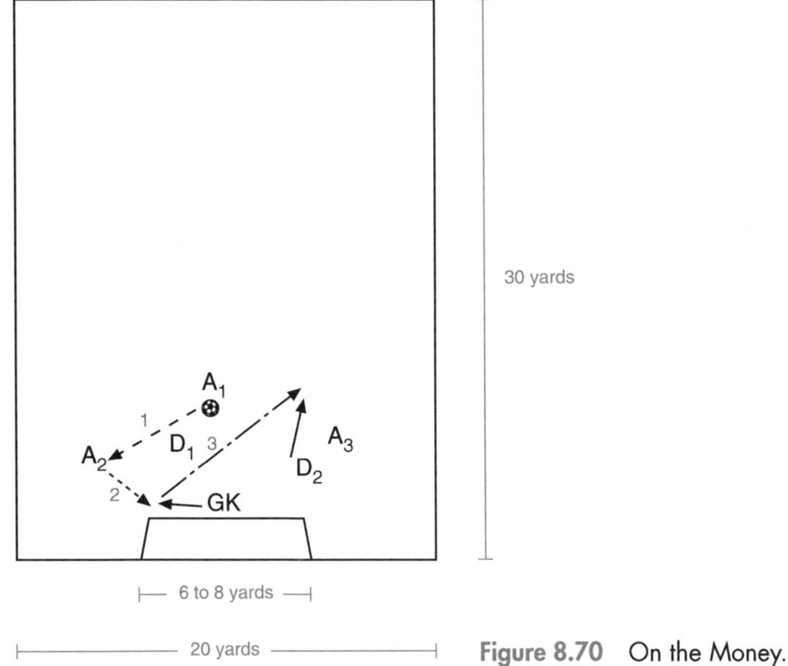

Figure 8.70 On the Money.

To make the game easier

- Play 2v3 or 2v4.

To make the game harder

- Add a point for a distribution that is successfully received and controlled beyond 15 yards for younger players and 20 yards for older players.

OVER THE TOP

Goal

To develop the ability to distribute the ball by punting it

Description

Play 3v3 in a 20- × 60-yard area. Use cones to mark three 20-yard zones within the 60-yard length of the field (see figure 8.71). The three players on offense attack the goal; they have no goalkeeper. The three on defense (including a goalkeeper) defend the goal. The defense scores in this manner:

(continued)

Over the Top *(continued)*

- 1 point for a shot stopped and successfully distributed by the goalie by punting the ball if the ball lands within zone 2 (the middle 20 yards)
- 2 points for a shot stopped and successfully distributed by the goalie by punting the ball if the ball lands within zone 3 (the farthest 20 yards)
- 1 additional point for any punt that is controlled by one of the goalie's teammates

Each player on defense gets three chances to punt; then flip-flop offense and defense.

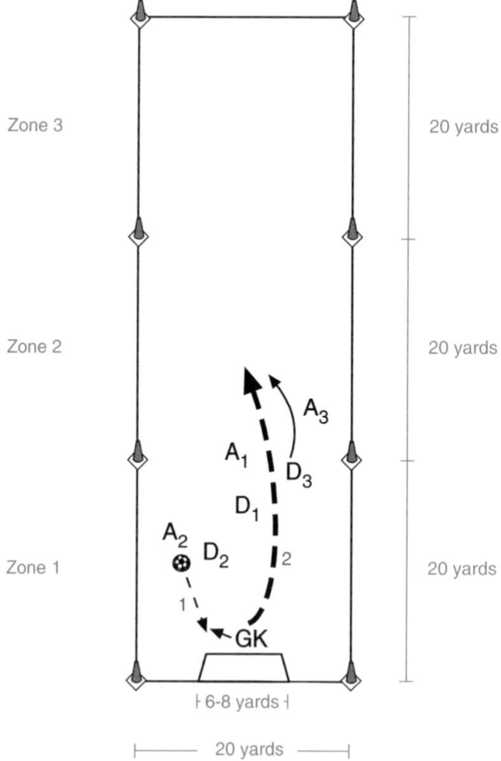

Figure 8.71 Over the Top.

To make the game easier

- Reduce the length of the field.
- Instruct the offense to kick the ball easily to the goalie to begin play and not to try to score a goal.

To make the game harder

- Give goalies a point for catching the ball cleanly.
- Increase the length of the field.

WHAT'S THE SCOOP?

Goal

To develop the ability to gather ground balls

Description

Play 2v1 in a 20- × 20-yard area with one goal (6 yards wide for younger players and 8 yards wide for older players; see figure 8.72). Two attackers try to score on one goalkeeper. The attackers take five shots on goal, passing between themselves and trying to get the best shot possible. The goalie gets 2 points for a "clean scoop" (one in which he or she cleanly gathers the ball), and 1 point for a stop that is

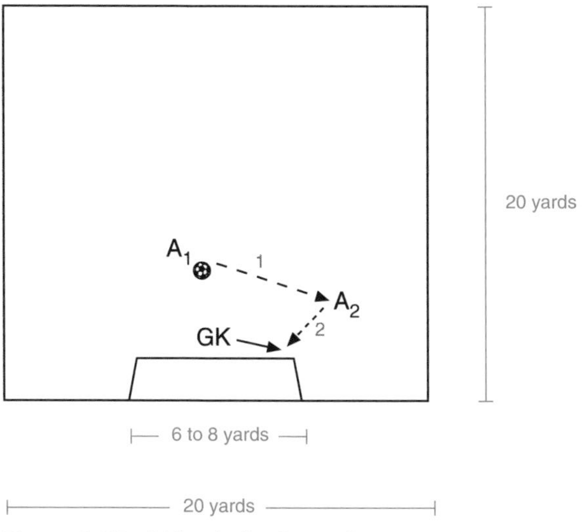

Figure 8.72 What's the Scoop?

(continued)

What's the Scoop? *(continued)*

not clean. The goalie gets no points if a goal is scored. To restart play the goalie tosses the ball back to the attackers. After every five chances to defend goal, rotate players so everyone gets to play goalie.

To make the game easier

- Increase the shot length.
- Decrease the speed of the shots.

To make the game harder

- Have players shoot to the corners.
- Increase the speed of the shots.

chapter 9

Season Plans

Hopefully you've learned a lot from this book: what your responsibilities as a coach are, how to communicate well and provide for safety, how to use the games approach to teach and shape skills, and how to coach on game days. But game days make up only a portion of your season—you and your players will spend more time in practice than in competition. How well you conduct practices and prepare your players for competition will greatly affect both your and your players' enjoyment and success throughout the season.

In this chapter, then, we present three season plans: one for 8- to 9-year-olds, one for 10- to 11-year-olds, and one for 12- to 14-year-olds. Use these plans as guidelines for conducting your practices. These plans are not the *only* way to approach your season, but they do present an appropriate teaching progression. Remember to incorporate the games approach as you use these plans.

The season plans have two components to them: purpose, and tactics and skills. By *purpose* we mean the overarching purpose of the particular practice—the main focus for that practice. *Tactics and skills* refer to the main tactics and skills that you will be teaching or refining during that practice. These tactics and skills will directly relate to the purpose for that practice. Other tactics and skills may come into play during the practice, but the ones we list are the ones that are integral to the purpose.

Good luck and good coaching!

Season Plan for 8- to 9-Year-Olds

Many 8- to 9-year-olds have had little or no exposure to soccer. Don't assume they have any knowledge of the game. Help them explore the basic tactics and skills of the sport, as suggested in the following season plan.

Practice	Purpose	Tactics and skills
1	To maintain possession and attack the goal through dribbling	Basic dribbling, both feet
2	To defend in 1v1 situations through marking	Marking (positioning; delaying attacker)
3	To attack the goal through shooting	Shooting
4	To maintain possession through receiving	Receiving the ball with the inside and outside of the foot
5	To maintain possession and attack through passing	Short passes
6	To attack by using the give-and-go	Give-and-go play
7	To defend in 1v1 situations through tackling	Block tackling
8	To defend goal through goalkeeping	Narrowing the angle; gathering ground balls; gathering air balls
9	To defend in 1v1 situations through tackling	Poke tackling

10	To maintain possession by providing support	Providing support; moving to open areas
11	To maintain possession and attack through passing	Short passes in combination play near the goal
12	To maintain possession through receiving	Receiving the ball with the thigh and chest
13	To attack the goal through shooting	Shooting
14	To attack the goal through corner kicks	Corner kicks

Season Plan for 10- to 11-Year-Olds

This season plan builds upon the previous one as players practice and refine the fundamental tactics and skills.

Practice	Purpose	Tactics and skills
1	To maintain possession and attack in 1v1 situations	Dribbling; basic moves to beat a defender
2	To defend in 1v1 situations through tackling	Block tackling; delaying and timing tackles
3	To maintain possession and attack in 2v1 situations	Providing support; moving to open areas; making lead passes
4	To maintain possession through receiving	Receiving the ball with the thigh and chest
5	To attack the goal through shooting	Shooting; receiving balls from the left or right before shooting
6	To maintain possession and attack through passing	Short passes in play near the goal

7	To maintain possession by providing support	Providing support in 3v1 or 4v2 games
8	To defend in 1v1 situations through tackling	Poke tackling; timing and execution of tackles
9	To defend in 2v2 situations	Marking and tackling; role of the second player in defending
10	To attack by using the give-and-go	Give-and-go play
11	To attack by making long passes	Long passes
12	To maintain possession by receiving and shielding	Receiving; shielding the ball
13	To defend the goal through goalkeeping	Distributing the ball by punting, rolling, and throwing
14	To attack the goal through corner kicks	Corner kicks

Season Plan for 12- to 14-Year-Olds

At this stage players are refining the skills they have learned from past years. This season plan builds upon the previous one and adds a few new skills, including heading and diving and collapsing for goalkeepers.

Practice	Purpose	Tactics and skills
1	To maintain possession and attack in 1v1 situations	Dribbling; beating the defender
2	To attack in 2v1 situations	Passing; give-and-go; providing support
3	To defend in 1v1 situations through tackling	Block and poke tackling

4	To attack the goal through corner kicks	Corner kicks
5	To attack the goal through shooting	Shooting; finishing balls low into corners
6	To attack the goal through heading	Heading
7	To defend in 2v2 situations	Marking and tackling; role of the second player in defending
8	To maintain possession by providing support	Providing support in 3v1 or 4v2 games
9	To defend in 3v3 situations	Marking and tackling; role of the third player in defending
10	To maintain possession through receiving	Receiving the ball with the thigh and chest
11	To maintain possession by receiving and shielding	Receiving; shielding the ball just outside the penalty area
12	To defend against corner kicks	Defending against corner kicks
13	To attack by making long passes	Long passes
14	To defend goal through goalkeeping	Diving and collapsing

Injury Report

Name of athlete ____

Date ______________________

Time ______________________

First aider (name) ____

Cause of injury ____

____

Type of injury ____

Anatomical area involved ______________________________________

Extent of injury ____

____

____

First aid administered ____

____

____

Other treatment administered ___________________________________

____

____

____

Referral action ____

____

____

____

____

First aider (signature)

Emergency Information Card

Athlete's name ______________________________ Age __________

Address ____

Phone ______________________ S.S.# ______________________

Sport ______________________

List two persons to contact in case of emergency:

Parent or guardian's name ______________________________

Address ____

Home phone ________________ Work phone ________________

Second person's name __________________________________

Address ____

Home phone ________________ Work phone ________________

Relationship to athlete ________________________________

Insurance co. ______________________ Policy # ____________

Physician's name ____________________ Phone ____________

IMPORTANT

Is your child allergic to any drugs? _____ If so, what? ________________

Does your child have any other allergies? (e.g., bee stings, dust) __________

Does your child suffer from ____ asthma, ____ diabetes, or ____ epilepsy?

Is your child on any medication? _______ If so, what? ________________

Does your child wear contacts? _____

Is there anything else we should know about your child's health or physical condition? If yes, please explain. ______________________________

____

____

____

____

______________________________ ____________________

Signature Date

Emergency Response Card

Information for emergency call
(Be prepared to give this information to the EMS dispatcher)

1. Location ______________________________

   Street address ______________________________

   City or town ______________________________

   Directions (cross streets, landmarks, etc.) ______________________________

   ____

   ____

2. Telephone number from which call is being made ______________________________
3. Caller's name ______________________________
4. What happened ______________________________

   ____

   ____

   ____

   ____

   ____

5. How many persons injured ______________________________
6. Condition of victim(s) ______________________________
7. Help (first aid) being given ______________________________

   ____

   ____

   ____

Note: Do not hang up first. Let the EMS dispatcher hang up first.